LEADERSHIP AND THE NURSE
An Introduction to the Principles of Management

* Also available as paperbacks

LEADERSHIP AND THE NURSE

An Introduction to the Principles of Management

MARGARET SCHURR, S.R.N.

THE ENGLISH UNIVERSITIES PRESS LTD
ST. PAUL'S HOUSE, WARWICK LANE
LONDON E.C.4

First printed 1968

SBN 340 05022 5

*Printed and bound in Great Britain for the English Universities Press Ltd
by Northumberland Press Ltd, Gateshead*

EDITORS' FOREWORD

THE MODERN NURSING SERIES
The aim of this series is to provide a comprehensive range of text-books and manuals written specially for students of nursing, midwifery, physiotherapy, radiography, speech training and medical social work. In assembling these texts care has been taken to maintain a reasonably uniform level of presentation with theory and practice kept in balance. Terminology is as rational as possible, and where necessary simple definitions of technical terms are included.

The series is designed to cover the requirements of the State Registration Examinations conducted by the General Nursing Council. It also includes books which cater for the needs of those who, while still at school, wish to prepare themselves for subsequent careers in nursing or in any of the ancillary medical professions.

As far as possible, each book will be written by a physician or surgeon in conjunction with a nursing sister or sister-tutor. This is with the deliberate intention of stressing the close association between clinical medicine and nursing.

Yet another aim of the series is, by ensuring that each book is of a handy size and weight, to enable them to find their way easily into the very centre of hospital practice as a kind of bench book.

THIS BOOK
Miss Schurr is a member of a medical family and trained as a nurse at University College Hospital. Previously Matron of a busy general hospital in a Teaching Group, and more recently a Nursing Officer in the Ministry of Health, she has had much experience of the special aspect of nursing with which this book is concerned.

Nurses are now accustomed to working as part of a team, be it a nursing team, a specialised unit, or a group of wards allocated to a speciality within a hospital. Nurses as matrons play their part in the day-to-day management of hospitals, groups of hospitals and nurse training schools. At whatever level a nurse works, she may be the "nurse-in-charge", a quotation from that great nurse and administrator Florence Nightingale.

This is an informative and up-to-date book which tackles the human and technical administrative problems which tend to concern all nurses.

It is a book for which the Salmon Report of the Committee on Senior Nursing Staff Structure has clearly seen an urgent need. All nurses will find it an understanding, helpful and stimulating companion.

A. J. HARDING RAINS
MARY CARPENTER

PREFACE

THE Nursing profession is aware of the need to study the principles of management, and emphasis has been given to the importance of management training in the Report of the Salmon Committee. How this can best be done has yet to be discovered, but whatever plans are made they will be fruitless unless those who attend Courses are able to apply the knowledge they acquire to their own situation.

This book has been written primarily to help nurses in First Line, and Middle Management. Not all the examples will be applicable to both groups, but the underlying principles are the same, and it has therefore been considered worthwhile to look at the responsibilities of the Nurse-in-Charge at both these levels. Illustrations have been confined to the hospital, but do not refer to any particular one, nor to any of the staff.

An attempt has also been made to show that the qualities of leadership are equally important, and that unless these are developed the most efficient management cannot succeed.

In the writing of this book, considerable use has been made of the material available in libraries and journals; and suggestions for further study have been included to encourage readers to search for themselves. In so doing, and by following up the references, they will broaden their knowledge and intellectual understanding. Wide reading must be an essential part of any programme directed towards post-certificate education.

Nurses are in contact with people all the time, whether it be at the bedside, working with colleagues in the School of Nursing, or at the Committee table, and some of the greatest discoveries which still have to be made lie in the field of communication and human relationships. It is hoped that what is found in these pages will help towards better understanding, and encourage a corporate feeling of responsibility among nurses in authority towards those whom they lead. There is a common goal, therefore the journey towards it must be shared. Only in this way will nurses achieve their ultimate purpose of providing the best possible care for patients.

MARGARET SCHURR

Garnett College of Education
for Teachers in Further Education, London, S.W.15.

vii

ACKNOWLEDGEMENTS

In recording my appreciation of those who have assisted me in the writing of this book, the general editors of this nursing series, and the staff of the English Universities Press, I should particularly like to thank Professor A. J. Harding Rains who first encouraged me to put pen to paper, and has consistently given his support.

I am also indebted to the Editor of the *Nursing Times* for permission to quote from articles in the nursing press, and to the following publishers for allowing references to their publications: Sir Isaac Pitman & Sons Ltd. for the reproduction of Fig. 7.1. of R. M. Currie's book *Work Study*, also for quotation from Colonel Urwick's book *Elements of Administration*; Jonathan Cape Ltd., for the extract from the *Life of Alexander Fleming* by André Maurois, translated by Gerard Hopkins.

Finally, I should like to thank all, who by their example, and their wisdom, have helped me to understand more fully the essentials of good leadership, and have encouraged me now to try to explain them to others.

CONTENTS

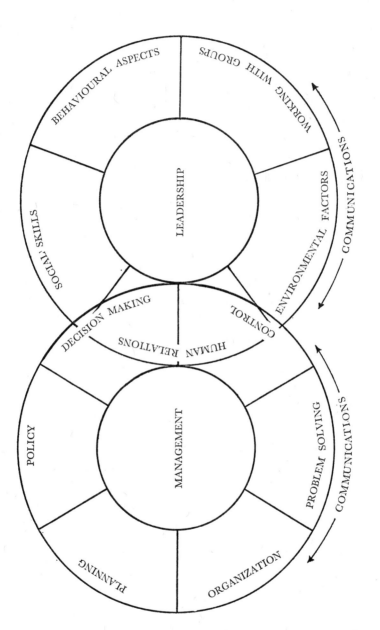

"The purpose and function of management cannot be separated from that of leadership"

PART ONE

POLICY PLANNING
AND
ORGANISATION

Let whoever is in charge keep this simple question in her
head, not how can I always do the right thing myself.
but how can I provide that the right thing shall always
be done.

Florence Nightingale

THE PURPOSE AND FUNCTION OF A HOSPITAL NURSING SERVICE

1. To provide a nursing service for patients and translate the instructions of the medical staff into action according to the highest professional standards.
   This provision must be consistent with the policies laid down by the governing body.

2. To define the objectives, principles and standards which govern the nursing care of patients, and ensure that these are consciously accepted and understood.

3. To provide and implement a pattern of administrative authority which enables all members of the nursing team to be aware of their individual duties and responsibilities.

4. To ensure free lines of communication which will assist the nursing team in their work; and provide a means whereby they can put forward their views and feel they are making a worthwhile contribution.

5. To estimate the requirements of the nursing service, and participate in all endeavours directed towards its improvement; reviewing established practices regularly, and making suggestions for change and development.

6. To participate in educational programmes for nurses and provide opportunities both for clinical experience, and the acquisition of knowledge which will improve the quality of the service.

7. To co-ordinate the activities of the nursing service with the function of the hospital as a whole.

8. To interpret the aims and objects of the nursing service to management, and also to the community.

PART ONE

POLICY PLANNING
AND
ORGANISATION

Let whoever is in charge keep this simple question in her head, not how can I always do the right thing myself. but how can I provide that the right thing shall always be done.

Florence Nightingale

THE PURPOSE AND FUNCTION OF A HOSPITAL NURSING SERVICE

1. To provide a nursing service for patients and translate the instructions of the medical staff into action according to the highest professional standards.
   This provision must be consistent with the policies laid down by the governing body.

2. To define the objectives, principles and standards which govern the nursing care of patients, and ensure that these are consciously accepted and understood.

3. To provide and implement a pattern of administrative authority which enables all members of the nursing team to be aware of their individual duties and responsibilities.

4. To ensure free lines of communication which will assist the nursing team in their work; and provide a means whereby they can put forward their views and feel they are making a worthwhile contribution.

5. To estimate the requirements of the nursing service, and participate in all endeavours directed towards its improvement; reviewing established practices regularly, and making suggestions for change and development.

6. To participate in educational programmes for nurses and provide opportunities both for clinical experience, and the acquisition of knowledge which will improve the quality of the service.

7. To co-ordinate the activities of the nursing service with the function of the hospital as a whole.

8. To interpret the aims and objects of the nursing service to management, and also to the community.

CHAPTER 1

LEADERSHIP AND MANAGEMENT

THROUGHOUT history there have been people who have taken their place as leaders in the community or in their own special field of work. Nursing is no exception, and the profession can be proud of the pioneers and those who have faithfully striven to maintain high standards of service. They have enabled nurses to enjoy a place of affection and respect in both this and other countries.

It is only recently, that attention has been paid to the nurse's role as a manager.[1,2] The complexity of hospital life has made it essential that nurses understand the principles which govern the art of administration. It is apparent that these principles need to be understood not only by those in the more senior positions in the nursing service, but by all who are "in charge" and in any way responsible for the welfare of others. They will be exercising leadership in their own sphere of activity at whatever level.

The purpose and function of management cannot be separated from that of leadership; and since nursing is essentially concerned with people, it would be wrong to consider the responsibilities of the nurse in charge without linking scientific knowledge and management skills very closely with the art of human relations.

What then is the purpose of leadership? To some it means the exercise of authority and the use of power in order to obtain personal prestige and reward. The true leader does not claim this for himself by virtue of his position, but realises that status is earned, and that allegiance comes when he has gained the confidence and respect of those for whom he is responsible. Leadership does not consist of stepping out in front hoping that the rest will follow, but in giving support from behind, enabling people to fulfil themselves and achieve their goals in an atmosphere of goodwill.

QUALITIES OF LEADERSHIP

Whilst it is true that those in authority can be trained and educated for their task, they must have certain basic qualities, which can be developed. A man or woman is not naturally a leader because he or she is exceptionally skilled at a job, although a sound technical knowledge is essential.

I. BASIC QUALITIES

(i) *Understanding.* There must be a readiness to understand

3

people; why they react in different ways, and have diverse needs. This means the giving of self, time, and energy in order to study human nature, and the impact which the environment makes upon each one of us. Every individual has a dignity of his own, and therefore people matter.

(*ii*) *Ability to Enlist Co-operation.* The striving, planning, and working towards a common goal must be a united effort based on mutual respect. The ideas and contributions of everyone must be welcomed in order to achieve an atmosphere of goodwill. Some people will need encouragement if they are to partake, but they must be made to feel that their contribution, however humble, is wanted.

(*iii*) *Ability to Communicate.* This quality is sufficiently important to warrant a section, Part II, devoted entirely to the subject. Communication is a two-way process, and although it is necessary to talk and be understood, it is just as necessary to listen.

(*iv*) *Ability to Delegate.* Those who cannot delegate will never be successful leaders. Not only do they become overwhelmed and incapable of performing their true function, they also deprive others of opportunity and of finding satisfaction in their work.

(*v*) *Wisdom.* Wise judgement, and the ability to make decisions is vital, and justice can never be separated from judgement. The leader will need courage, and must not shrink from questioning the validity of an issue. Then, having obtained the facts, she* must have the wisdom to discriminate. She must accept that she cannot know all the answers, but that she can know where and how to seek help, and be prepared to accept this willingly and graciously.

II. PERSONAL QUALITIES
  (*i*) *Beliefs and Values.* The personality of the individual will influence the quality of the leadership. Beliefs, values, and inspiration, are part of the make-up of people, and can influence the whole of their lives and conduct.

(*ii*) *Integrity.* Character consists of many things, but integrity is essential in those who are in any way responsible for others. It must be known and proved that they can be trusted in all situations. It is often this, and not the position held in the hierarchy which will command the respect of those who are led. They appreciate a natural sincerity and consistency which means that they will not be let down.

  * Although the female pronoun is used, the masculine can equally apply throughout this narrative.

(*iii*) *Moral Courage and Determination.* It has been said that people learn to trust those who prove themselves. When they see moral courage in action, they take note. They recognise the ability and determination which guides and controls a difficult situation, and will acknowledge the person who will stand by them through a time of testing. One of the most important functions of a leader is to support in times of stress, giving the encouragement and sympathy that is needed in order to progress through a period of trial or strain. In the hospital the nurse in charge has such an opportunity when she gives her support to the student nurse who meets the problem of incurable disease in a young patient for the first time.

(*iv*) *Self-control and Self-respect.* The leader who has learnt to understand herself is in a position to exercise self-control. This understanding does not mean introspection, but the ability to recognise a weakness, and to be sufficiently humble to acknowledge it, and take action. The person who can do this will possess poise and serenity which in turn produces self-respect.

(*v*) *Sense of Humour.* A sense of humour is a great asset. Leadership should be enjoyed, and any contact with people holds with it the possibility of happiness—always depending on how the person looks at the situation. There are, of course, times when a sense of humour is out of place, but there are few occasions which cannot be lightened by a cheerful countenance, and frequently there is room for optimism. A certain amount of vivacity and enjoyment of life must come through if other people are to feel that their contribution is worthwhile.

If all these qualities are considered together, they will be found in a person whose character is one of harmony: someone who possesses, through self knowledge and appreciation of the needs of others, a balanced objective outlook which can control and direct a situation, and bring out the best in them.

PREPARATION FOR LEADERSHIP

The nursing profession has sometimes been a little slow in spotting potential leaders at an early date, and it is possible that some of the failure to find sufficent people to fill responsible posts today, is because they were not sought among the ranks of yesterday.

There is already one branch of the National Health Service which employs "planned movement". This is a means of providing personnel with opportunities to prepare for positions of responsibility. Particular members of staff have their careers mapped out in a progressive pattern so that if they come up to expectation; they are able to reach a position of leadership more quickly.

Nurses must consider the wisdom of taking the trouble to seek for those with qualities of leadership and give them the opportunity to gain the necessary experience and training to equip them for further responsibility. Sometimes there may be a reluctance to give praise where it is due, and the encouragement which may make all the difference when a colleague or a trainee is deciding on future plans.

Serious thought must also be given to the training and education of leaders. This is a subject for the profession to consider with the help of the educationalists. Much can be learnt from Industry, and from other disciplines which have given thought to the subject and have made considerable progress.

There is one aspect, however, to which all nurses can make a contribution; namely to produce within the hospital an environment in which these potential leaders can grow. In the following chapters an attempt will be made to show how this can be done, remembering always that some of the best teaching and training will always be by example.

REFERENCES

[1] Report of the Committee on the Senior Nursing Staff Structure, Ministry of Health and Scottish Home and Health Department. H.M.S.O.

[2] *Administering the Hospital Nursing Service*. A Review. Royal College of Nursing and National Council of Nurses.

SUGGESTION FOR FURTHER READING

The Art of Leadership, by Ordway Tead. Published by Whiltlesey House, Division of McGraw Hill Book Co., New York and London.

SUGGESTION FOR FURTHER STUDY

It has been said that "It is the responsibility of Management to lead". Prepare notes for a discussion on this statement.

CHAPTER 2

DEFINING A POLICY

MANAGEMENT has been described as the process of "initiating, organising and controlling group activity directed to the achievement of certain objectives".[1] What is the significance of this for the nurse who is in the position of manager?

Firstly, she must know and understand the objectives. Every organisation, whether it is an Industrial concern, or a Hospital, must have an ultimate goal, and a philosophy which will support its achievement. The Directors of a Company concentrate on quality and productivity so that they may obtain satisfied customers. They pay attention to the training of their managers so that factories, workshops and offices will function smoothly, and the employees will be contented.

The aim of the hospital, is to provide the highest possible standard of care for patients, and thus enable them to return home in as good a state of health as possible. This could be termed "profit by results". If the objective is to become a reality, able managers will also be required, and the staff must find satisfaction and happiness in their work.

The Oxford Dictionary describes policy as "a plan to achieve certain ends". Those responsible for management, therefore, must have a well defined policy to guide them towards their goal. In the hospital service this is decided by governing bodies at regional and local level. Some examples and the diagram on page 8 may prove helpful.

EXAMPLES

Stage A. The Board of Governors or Regional Board agree with the Ministry of Health that a Hospital will provide all the functions of a District General Hospital, including an Accident Service. This hospital will also be a Regional Centre for Neurosurgery. There will be training for nurses for both the Register and the Roll, and an arrangement with the local Psychiatric Hospital for a combined scheme to enable nurses to qualify for the general and psychiatric registers. The Teaching Hospital will, of course, have a Medical School.

Stage B. The Board of Governors for the Teaching Hospital, and the Hospital Management Committee for the non-teaching, have

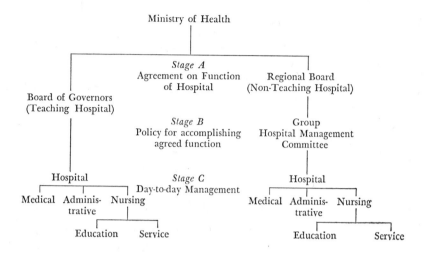

the responsibility of providing these services, and the training requirements. A financial allocation is made to them, and they decide how the money is to be spent. They agree on the staffing establishments, provision of medical care, number of consultant sessions, etc. They maintain accommodation for patients and staff, and agree a policy concerning the number and grades who are required to live within the precincts of the hospital; keeping in mind the facilities for obtaining suitable houses and flats in the area.

Stage C. Medical and Nursing specialists who care for the patients know how many can be satisfactorily treated. This will depend partly on the length of stay, but may be influenced by the quality of nursing care which is available. In the case of the Neurosurgical Unit, therefore, the ratio of staff to patients will be assessed, and the policy for the organisation and content of the nursing team will be carefully planned. The Hospital Secretary will be concerned with the provision of catering and ancillary staff and the supporting services. It is therefore essential that there is frequent consultation between the lay administration and the heads of the medical and nursing teams.

MAKING POLICY DECISIONS EFFECTIVE

If they are to produce results, policy decisions must be realistic and be founded on fact. They must reflect the opinions of those who execute them, and these people should be consulted so that they are able to make their contribution. Policy made in isolation can be most harmful. Suppose that in a hospital, steps are taken to alter the number of paediatric beds without conferring with the Nursing Administration and the Principal Tutor. It could happen that these were reduced so as to make it impossible to give all the clinical experience required by the nurses in training. The specialists in each area of the hospital must be prepared to put forward their views without hesitation, in order to avoid misjudgements, and to help those with ultimate control to act with wisdom.

THE CONTRIBUTION OF THE NURSE-IN-CHARGE

This account of policy-making at management committee level may seem to have digressed from the original problem of how the nurse is to get to know their objectives. It is, however, relevant, and the nurse-in-charge must be familiar with the activities and structure of hospital management so that she may apply this knowledge when planning the work of the group with which she is concerned.

EXAMPLE

The Departmental Sister in control of the Regional Neuro-surgical Unit must know that the Regional Board have agreed to accept patients from the surrounding district. She must also know how many beds there are to be, and, with the assistance of medical colleagues, plan their use to the best advantage. She will advise those in control of the nursing service on the numbers and grades of nursing staff required so that the Hospital Management Committee may be informed. This will depend on the plan she has adopted for the nursing of the patients—whether it is thought advisable to group them in a pattern of progressive patient care, and whether or not there will be a system of internal rotation of staff for night duty. These plans will affect the facilities for clinical experience for the nurses in training, and she will therefore have discussions with the Principal of the School of Nursing.

It may be useful at this juncture, to clarify the steps which are necessary when seeking to decide the policy which will govern a course of action.

1. Determine the purpose—what is the ultimate aim?
2. Look ahead and try to anticipate the future (Forecasting).
3. Look back and see what has been happening.
4. Look at the present situation.
5. Collect this information together, sort out the relevant material, and assemble it in an orderly fashion.
6. Decide on the course of action, making sure it achieves the objective—and is necessary.

CRITERIA FOR DECISION MAKING

The Past

Accumulated Knowledge
Past experience
Where and why were
modifications made?
Statistics
References

The Present

What is happening now?
   Why?
      How?
         When?
            Where?
Is this evidence valid?
What is the effect on
   people?
     their work?
       the ultimate purpose?

*CONSULTATION
AND
DISCUSSION*

RESEARCH

The Future

What could happen?
  Why?
    How?
      When?
        Where?

COLLECTED INFORMATION
  sorting
  assembling

DECISION

DETERMINING THE PURPOSE

Nurses who are in close touch with patients in the ward or department will have little doubt concerning the purpose of their work. It may, however, be more difficult for the Senior Nurse Administrator who is dealing with wider issues which affect the quality of the nursing service and the welfare of the individuals who give it.

EXAMPLES

I. Several requests are made to the Head of the Nursing Service by married nurses for annual leave during the school holidays. It would be easy to accede to this in the interests of the nurses and their children. However, this could mean a shortage of people to look after the patients during specific periods. A policy must therefore be worked out that will keep the number of staff available for duty within reasonable limits, and also give fair consideration to the problems of the married nurse.

II. Supposing that a hostel for student nurses is to be opened in a new hospital. Many people will consider that the immediate step will be to appoint a Warden to be in charge. This would be unwise, since the first consideration must be the overall management of the hostel. The policy for this should be inextricably bound up with that for the education of the nurses. Education is not only the acquisition of knowledge. It includes the development of character and preparation for life so that the individual may take her place as a responsible citizen. The overall aim, therefore, must be to encourage the students themselves to be responsible for the maintenance of discipline. There will be a reference to this later under another heading, but it emphasises the importance of considering the wider implications, and of being sure of the ultimate goal. Having considered these aspects, it will be easier to decide upon the type of person required when appointing the Warden.

LOOKING AHEAD

It is a gift to be able to predict and determine future trends, but everyone can contribute to some extent by using previous experience. The future can be viewed in the broad perspective of the present and the past. This means standing outside the situation and trying to be completely objective. It is easy to become involved, and then thoughts become distorted by what is felt at the particular moment. This tendency has to be overcome.

LOOKING BACK

This is sometimes easier than looking ahead. At the least there are some facts to work on. It is wise, however, to remember that events of the past become modified and changed when in retrospect, and that it is a human failing to add to the experience. A fair estimation of the past is therefore imperative, and as much help as possible should be sought in order to collect accurate information.

LOOKING AT THE PRESENT

It would clearly be wrong to consider a proposed course of action without considering the present situation, and it has already been stressed that it is important in order to be objective.

Another illustration may help to show how necessary this "wide viewing" can be.

EXAMPLE

A Ward Sister has been asked to consider supporting staff for the nursing team, and it has been suggested that the domestic and "hotel" duties should be undertaken by a Ward Housekeeper with her own staff. Sister will need to think about the general policy for the ward administration in the light of this suggestion. Some of the following questions could help her to come to a decision.

1. *Looking Ahead*
   a. The main purpose is to give the best possible care to the patients. Would this suggestion improve or hinder this care?
   b. If this help were provided, would there be an improvement in the general ward administration? Would the nurses have more time to be with the patients?
   c. How would the introduction of another grade of staff affect the patients, the training of nurses, the general ward routine, and the domestic staff?
   d. Would there be a need to change the pattern of patient care to, for instance, Group assignment?

2. *Looking Back*
   Are the nurses undertaking tasks which others could do? Have some of the duties in the past been handed on by tradition without any re-consideration? (A list of these duties could be helpful.)

3. *Looking at the Present*
   a. Are nurses in training receiving adequate supervision?
   b. Are the senior staff free to be with the patients and nurses, or is too much time spent on "housekeeping" which could be delegated?
   c. Are there any recent instances which have shown that the ward administration could be improved?

There will be many more questions which can be asked, and

members of the ward team should join in. Underlying all this thinking will be the welfare of the patient. It is obvious that if the Ward Sister is going to measure the advantages of this additional help against the present situation, she must be quite sure about the standard of care which she wishes to achieve for the patients. One of the yardsticks will be to consider what she would wish for herself or for her own relatives. It is useful for all doctors and nurses, particularly when in training, to think of the care of the patients with whom they are associated in this context. There are, of course, not only physical comfort and good technique to be considered, but also the attitudes of the staff towards their patients, and towards their colleagues.

Constructive thinking along these lines will ensure that there will be appreciable headway towards knowing what the policy is to be.

COLLECTING THE INFORMATION

This is an art, but when it is considered that the validity of the decision will depend on ability in this direction, it is worthwhile taking time and trouble.

Information can be obtained from any or all of the following:

1. People concerned with the work and administration who can assist by their knowledge of present and past circumstances.
2. Specialists who can assist by their particular knowledge or interest.
3. Standing Committees who can be asked for advice.
4. Other organisations faced with similar problems.
5. Records and historical references.
6. Literature which defines current policy.
7. Questionnaires.
8. Personal investigation.

The usefulness of questionnaires is limited unless they are very carefully constructed so that the information received is of value. Answers will only be obtained to specific inquiries, and the questions must be framed so that ambiguous replies are reduced to a minimum.

Personal investigation has been placed at the end of the list not because it is the least important, for it can be of the utmost value. It is true, however, that the amount of information obtained depends very much on the type of personal approach and the manner of questioning.

Having collected the material it then has to be sorted. It is helpful to group the facts under different headings, putting them into two categories—those for, and those against, the proposal. It is a good plan to make a final check to ensure that the details are as correct and complete as possible before taking the final step.

MAKING THE DECISION

Having collected the facts, the policy which appears to be the correct one must be reconciled with the resources which are available. Can this be achieved? In so doing, will the standards be maintained and the most cherished values survive? It was Fredrike Münster of the Kaiserswerth Nursing School who warned "never to sacrifice the soul of the work for its technique!"

There was an article written by an administrator some years ago which illustrates the wisdom of these words. It describes a hospital secretary of considerable ability and efficiency who much impressed the Management Committee. He turned his attention to the Group administration, determined to streamline procedures and provide everyone with a neat schedule of their duties. He employed all the scientific tools of management, and among them a work-study exercise of the portering system. The story goes on to describe how, although the staff co-operated to the best of their ability, some of them felt that all was not well. They were at a loss to know what was the matter until one day a Student Nurse asked a simple question: "Why," she asked, "don't the porters whistle any more?"[2] The creation of an efficient organisation is not enough—it must also be human.

The need for an unhurried decision has already been emphasised. An experienced leader will not try to reach conclusions at the end of a busy day, or when worried about another problem. Circumstances can look very different after a good night's sleep, and a period of quietness is necessary for some of the important decisions which must be made. Finally, having come to a conclusion, the leader must stand by it. This takes courage, but courage is one of the essentials of leadership.

MAKING THE PLAN

Having followed through this exercise, the nurse should be in a position to work out the plan which will interpret the agreed policy. Success will greatly depend on the degree of co-operation between herself and the group who will carry it out. The nurse is fortunate when she is surrounded by others who feel the same impulse and the necessity for the same goal. So much can be achieved by a few who are dedicated to the same end. It is much harder when people have to be convinced that the proposals are worthwhile, and it is easy to become disheartened when faced with opposition. It has been proved, however, that if a group gets together from the beginning, most of the members will co-operate and the minority opinion of the dissenters is less harmful. Since every situation is different, and since the principles which are adopted vary accordingly, it is not easy to give guidance on their interpretation. In most instances there will be need for some kind of change from the existing pattern—either from an established policy, or towards the acceptance of the new one. Preparation for this is so important that it will be considered as a separate subject in the next chapter.

REFERENCES

[1] W. R. Calvert, Principal of Department of Administrative Studies, H.M. Treasury.

[2] "Whistle Stop," C. A. S. Brooks, D.P.A.F.H.A., *British Hospital Journal and Social Service Review*, 10.11.61, page 1301.

SUGGESTION FOR FURTHER READING

Principles of Administration applied to the Nursing Service by H. A. Goddard. Published by World Health Organisation, Geneva 1958.

SUGGESTIONS FOR FURTHER STUDY

FOR SENIOR NURSE ADMINISTRATORS (MIDDLE MANAGEMENT)

1. Owing to a shortage of Technicians, qualified nurses in the Out-patient Department are taking intravenous blood samples in certain clinics. Consider the steps which should be taken to arrive at an agreed policy between medical and nursing personnel as to whether or not this duty should be undertaken by nurses.

2. Prepare a policy statement to present to the Hospital Management Committee for their approval in support of the introduction of a Shift System of duty for the Nursing Staff.

FOR WARD SISTERS, STAFF NURSES, SENIOR ENROLLED NURSES (FIRST LEVEL MANAGEMENT)

Consider instances whereby the ward administration has suffered from:

(a) Ignorance of the policy of the Hospital Management Committee.

(b) Failure of the medical officer and the nurse to come to an agreement on policy for the nursing care of patients.

(c) The Ward Sister failing to discuss policy with the nursing team.

CHAPTER 3

INTERPRETATION OF POLICY

PRESENTING THE PLAN AND INSTITUTING CHANGE

WHY make a change? It is often so much easier to leave things as they are. Changes can be very uncomfortable. They challenge security and well-established ideas and threaten the stronghold of traditions which have become as familiar as a part of life. A different pattern or outlook may uncover poor practice and remove the shelter behind which those who are not very sure of themselves have been protected.

On the other hand, it is important that the senior nurse should be on the alert to spot those occasions when a new approach will be an improvement. She needs to be constantly examining day-to-day activity in the light of changes going on around her, not only so that new ideas are brought in, but also to keep those in current use which are fresh, lively and challenging. There are four possible reasons for introducing change:

1. IN ORDER TO SOLVE A PROBLEM

Sometimes people are faced with a situation in which it is known that to suggest an adjustment or alteration to a certain method will cause distress and antagonism; and yet, it is obvious that the method is bad and extravagant of time and energy. This may be the right occasion to introduce something quite new rather than to make relatively minor alterations. The novelty, and the opportunity to try out a different method may appeal, whereas criticism of the old way would be quite unacceptable and just cause resentment. For instance, if a great deal of time is being spent in the wards writing up books about the patients' treatment, suggesting to the Ward Sister that she is the ideal person to experiment with a new kind of record card will not only secure her interest, but will probably solve the problem.

2. TO APPLY A PRINCIPLE

Inconsistency of any kind is undesirable, and it may be that having adopted a policy or principle, change will be inevitable. A simple example could occur over the question of the elimination of sources of infection. A committee is set up to control infection in the wards and departments. Their recommendations might include the introduction of several disposable items of equipment in order to improve standards, and then it is realised that the nursing staff are going to the dining-room in their aprons! This may produce quite a problem in cramped accommodation, but would justify a change if the principle is to be applied.

3. To Introduce Improvements

Suppose that a group of ward sisters is concerned that the continuous activity in their wards is making it difficult for the patients to have sufficient rest. They approach the medical staff and ask for their co-operation, suggesting that for one hour after lunch patients are left to sleep undisturbed. They change the pattern of the daily routine to make this possible. As a result of their decision, other ward sisters will follow the example, considering that the good results obtained will justify the necessary changes.

4. To Introduce New Ideas

When introducing new ideas, it is important to remember that an innovation in one situation may be quite unsuitable in another. Everyone is familiar with the enthusiast who reads about a particular piece of equipment in a weekly journal, and decides there and then that it is the answer to all problems. The article is purchased without sufficient consultation and assessment of its usefulness, and then it is found, either that it does not serve the purpose for which it was intended, or that the cost of maintenance is prohibitive. These are errors which hospitals cannot afford. It is far worse, however, when a change is made which adversely affects people and their way of life. New ideas imposed from above which are neither acceptable nor practicable can be damaging, and the repercussions far-reaching.

Provided as much care as possible has been taken in deciding on a course of action, it is best to adhere to it even if the unexpected occurs. It may be necessary to give way in some directions, since too much rigidity can ruin the whole plan. However, only minor adjustments which do not relinquish basic principles should be made. Nowadays there is much emphasis on the need for change, and there is a real danger of letting go institutions which are vital to professional performance. On the other hand, if a mistake has been made, it is far better to withdraw the plan before any damage is done, and then to find another approach.

Newcomers and Fresh Ideas

Mistakes often occur because an attempt has been made to introduce a change too quickly. On entering a new job, it is easy to be over-enthusiastic; coming with fresh ideas and insight, there is so much that appears to be in need of change. It is a good idea to have two mental lists—one for those things which cannot wait, as they urgently affect the good of the whole organisation, and the other for items which are desirable, but need not have priority. A third list may be required for those items which are desirable, but which cannot be implemented in the forseeable future. It is as well, however, to have this list at hand for the unexpected opportunity which may come.

When first undertaking a position of leadership, there is a danger that the situation will be assessed too rapidly. It takes time to get to know people, and the reasons for their actions, and some of the practices which appear to be faulty may, in fact, be done for a reason which has not yet been discovered. It is also true that it may be better to allow a barely adequate method to continue for a short time, rather than make an immediate change which will not be acceptable or will not be understood.

THE RIGHT MOMENT

Choosing the right time to introduce change is one of the most vital factors. Not only must there be a period in which to prepare, observe and correlate ideas, but the people who are to interpret the plan must be given time to adjust themselves to the individual who created it. They need to understand the kind of person they are dealing with and what is expected of them. It is important that actions are explained and justified in a language which all can understand. There must also be a period during which the plan can be assimilated and accepted. The wise leader will put the proposition to the group at the earliest opportunity, but will temporarily withdraw it if it is rejected. It sometimes happens that, over the course of weeks or even months, circumstances will arise which bring the suggestion back into the limelight—it may even come from someone else as their idea. If so, this is all to the good, for if people feel that they are responsible for the new project, they will give their energy to its success.

Occasionally, it is possible to introduce a new idea when it is topical. The publication of a Ministry of Health Memorandum or an article in the Nursing Press may give the opportunity for emphasising the need in a particular situation. Once attention is drawn to this, the necessary support will be forthcoming. An illustration comes to mind of a hospital where there is difficulty in getting the nursing staff of a children's ward to appreciate the need for frequent visiting by the parents. Instructions that this is to be done will probably not succeed if the principle is not accepted, but if advice comes from an authority outside the hospital, and is therefore not directed at one particular group, it has more chance of being appreciated.

When considering the time to introduce change, it is important to remember that the idea may not have a good reception if those who are being approached are themselves undergoing a time of stress. It may be wise to wait until this period is over and the staff can give their full attention to new ideas.

RESISTANCE TO CHANGE

It is worthwhile considering what action can be taken if there is resistance to change. "Mental barriers" as they may be called, usually appear because people are frightened. This is not always appreciated. The fear of loss of status, or of an inability to manage the new system, or even that the change will mean redundancy, may be standing in the way. This is less likely if the right preparation has been made, but insecurity can be a very real obstacle, and may be responsible for a rapid decline in efficiency.

Resistance may also be caused by lack of knowledge or interest. It is possible that those who will have to interpret a new plan are not sufficiently able, and in an effort to cover up their feeling of insufficiency find it easier to oppose the issue. This sometimes happens when a member of staff is nearing retirement and is asked to undertake a venture which needs considerable skill and exertion. Opposition in this case may really be due to a lack of physical energy, and in these circumstances it may be wrong to make the demand.

Sometimes there may be people who cannot be bothered, and find it more convenient to resist change. Occasionally their enthusiasm may be won by sending them to see another hospital or situation where the particular idea which is being advocated has been a success. However, it is essential to find the right people to talk to them, or more harm may be done than good.

Finally, progress and change can be hampered by authoritarian attitudes, and the existence of the hierarchy. A good plan may be accepted by the group, but is halted at a higher level. The only way to overcome this is by persistent pressing of the point, and confidence in the value of the proposition. When it is seen that the group feels sufficiently strongly that this is a useful contribution, and that they are not prepared to relinquish it, opposition may be overcome. However, it sometimes happens that those in authority, having the wide picture of the whole organisation, can see that a particular plan is not the right one and, if this occurs, their judgement must be accepted. It may be that having become aware of the further implications, the group can modify their ideas and make them acceptable.

SELLING IDEAS

It has already been stressed that it is unwise to force new suggestions upon other people. It is far better, if there is time, to guide the thoughts of the group over a longer period, so that ultimately the change is welcomed. Reasons for change must be explained most carefully, people have a right to know the reason why. The establishment of an Intensive Care Unit for patients may seem on the surface to be an unnecessary concentration of nursing skill, and the medical staff may not like the idea of having their patients away from their own particular ward. This is a situation where a clear explanation of the reasons behind the suggestion can help. There are few nurses who will deny that it is difficult to give supervision by qualified nurses and skilled care to seriously ill patients when they are distributed throughout the hospital; and that concentrating them in one area can result in better nursing. There are also few doctors who would not wish this special care to be available for their patients. Examples of situations when such provision would have been helpful may convince those who are doubtful. Gentle persuasion over the course of time can do great things.

New ideas are only acceptable if the people concerned can see that their leader has faith in the venture, and truly believes that it will be beneficial. Any lack of confidence can be quickly detected, making it easy to attack any weak points in the plan. It must be possible to substantiate ideas, and explain exactly what is required.

The amount of enthusiasm brought to the plans will also influence the degree of success. Someone who is dull, and lacks inspiration, is not going to carry people through a time of change. If the new plan can be seen as a challenge, this in itself will attract those seeking for adventure. It may help if a physical change is planned at the same time. It is a strange, but positive fact, that people react more favourably to new ideas if they coincide with a change in the environment—even if it is only new chaircovers and curtains.

Sometimes it is wise to approach only a small group in the first instance. There will always be those who share the responsibility of the nurse who is in charge, and who are closer to her in her work. By enlisting their co-operation first, it may be found that the task is done, and that they will spread the idea to the remainder of the team.

While this process is going on, it is important to be accessible. As the news travels, questions will be asked, and someone must be ready to answer them. It is necessary to anticipate the kind of questions which will be forthcoming, and so be prepared for any obstacles and difficulties. Informal discussions which bring the subject into the conversation can be very useful, and this will often win the confidence of a member of the team. Preconceived ideas which are wide of the mark may be standing in the way.

INITIAL EXPERIMENTATION

Even with the greatest care to ensure the acceptance of a new scheme, repercussions will be inevitable, and there will be a certain amount of anxiety about going forward with plans. On the other hand, there may be so many points in favour of the change that it would be unwise to drop the idea altogether. In these circumstances it is useful to try it first in one place as an experiment. There will probably be a group of people who are more receptive and amenable to new ideas and they can be approached. If this is done, however, it is most important to assess the results of the enterprise so that a decision can be made as to whether or not to pursue the whole exercise. It often happens that trials are done and nobody bothers to follow them up, so that much personal time and energy is wasted.

One person, or a small group should be appointed as assessor. Those who are chosen must be known to be fair in their judgement and must have sufficient knowledge to give a critical and objective survey of the situation. When their comments are available, there must be a full and frank discussion so that it is known where to expect difficulties, and where success. This is always providing a typical situation has been chosen, and not an atypical one. Certain allowances may have to be made for the circumstances in which the work has been undertaken, since experiments do not always go as expected. However, it is better to have failed in one small situation and to admit defeat, than to have launched into a new plan of some size which has involved many people, and then to come to grief.

On occasions, those in authority have been tempted to turn to an alternative plan as a matter of expediency when the original one has failed. This can be dangerous, since to accept a compromise at this juncture may bring endless trouble. An offer which will satisfy at the moment may be a stumbling block when circumstances have changed. Taking a long calm look at a time of defeat will help things to appear in a different light, and give fresh inspiration. This may be a turning point which will benefit many in the future.

THE CREATION OF A NEW PLAN

Many aspects of change have been considered, including some of the pitfalls which can jeopardise good ideas. It may be helpful, therefore, to summarise these and illustrate by an example.

1. Be ready to see the need for change and be sure that it is justified.

2. Remember the importance of choosing the right time.
3. Make the plans carefully—possibly by an experiment in a small area at first. Look ahead and see what has to be done and consider the resources available.
4. Know how to obtain the co-operation of the groups.
5. Explain the detail of the plan in a way which can be understood.
6. Be ready to evaluate the success or failure of the plan, and know what difficulties to expect and how to overcome them.

Need for Change

Justification
Timing
Obstacles

Discussion and Consultation

Making Plans
Description and Propaganda

Acceptance and Understanding

Experimentation   Evaluation

Decisions for Future

EXAMPLE

The suggestion is that an internal rota for night duty might be a welcome change in a busy district general hospital. The previous pattern has been a three-monthly tour of night duty, with three nights off duty weekly. There are some part-time nursing staff working two or three nights in addition.

1. *What is the need for this change?*

The trained nursing staff are concerned that those who undertake night duty are often unfamiliar with the ward situation. The hospital admits many emergencies, the work is acute and there are therefore many changes over the course of twenty-four hours. The relief nurses find it difficult to assimilate all that they must know with the pace of the work at night, and to adapt to a different ward at frequent intervals. The Nurse Tutors and Administrators are worried about the amount of night duty undertaken by third year student nurses in particular. The suggestion of internal night duty is made, but has to be abandoned because of shortage of staff, there not being a sufficient number to form the "pool" which is necessary for the scheme to work.

Several months pass and there is an increase in the number of state registered and state enrolled nurses, and nursing auxiliaries. The situation is therefore much better, but the student nurses are still being required to do more than their share of night duty under the present system.

CONSULTATION AND DISCUSSION

The Staff Nurses refer to this at the Nurses Representative Council, and one of them describes an article in the current issue of the Nursing Press which refers to internal night duty. It is agreed that this should be discussed with the various groups, and that the senior nursing staff should consider the matter at their next meeting. The Student Nurses are asked to think this over, and to have some comments ready if the suggestion is followed up.

A busy time ensues whilst Tutors and Nurse Administrators discuss the implications with the night and day Sisters. The Sisters take the matter up with their own ward teams, and all the implications are considered. At this point they are concerned mainly with the effect on nursing care, and secondly with the wellbeing of the staff. The actual plan is not produced, but a rough estimate is made to be sure that the suggestion is a practicable one. The points in favour are as follows:

a. Service to patients should improve—nurses would be familiar with their needs after having been in the ward previously on day duty. This would relieve the Night and Day Sisters of much anxiety.
b. Night duty would be shared more equally, and the amount could be kept within the recommendations of the General Nursing Council.
c. The long periods of night duty at one time would cease.
d. Nurses could retain their own bedrooms throughout training.

There are certain points raised against the plan. Questions arise about the part-time nurses and how they will fit into the pattern. The general opinion is that the change would be justified.

2. *Choosing the Time*

It is the beginning of the year—an excellent time to organise the plan. It will take at least three months, but by April the bulk of the holidays will be over, and sickness should be less. A date is arranged for the second Monday in April.

3. *Making the Plan*
A Night Sister, Ward Sister, Nurse Tutor and a Nurse Administrator volunteer to produce some rotas for everyone to see. The Staff Nurses have a suggestion, and this will be put forward with the one from the Nursing Journal.
After considerable thought and discussion two possible rotas appear to be suitable. Both can be managed with the number of staff available, but one of them would require the staff nurses to take part. It will be remembered that their concern was for the nurses in training, and they did not include themselves in the original discussion.
Copies are made of the two patterns. It is important that the rota can be studied individually—at least on every ward; copies on notice boards are not satisfactory, or even circulating at a meeting, as there is not sufficient time to study in detail.

4. *Co-operation and Acceptance of the Plan*
This change will not only affect nurses, but will also have repercussions on other staff who supply services to the hospital. A list is therefore made of the people who will be affected.

1. Trained Nursing Staff.
2. Nurses in training.
3. Auxiliary staff—even if not partaking in the rota.
4. Medical Staff.
5. Catering Officer.
6. The Home Wardens.
7. Domestic Superintendent.
8. Hospital Secretary.

A report on progress will also need to be made to the House Committee and/or Nursing Committee.
The Nurse Administrator responsible for this new plan arranges for certain members of the team to undertake arrangements with the Catering and Domestic Officers, while she prepares a series of informal meetings with the nurses, and sees as many of the medical staff as possible to explain the need for the change. The Home Wardens welcome the suggestion.
A difficulty arises during the meeting with the Staff Nurses. They feel that the rota which involves themselves is possibly the better one, but they are not all prepared to partake. They do not feel they should be asked to do regular night duty periods once

qualified. The Nurse Administrator who is chairing the meeting realises that this is not a unanimous opinion, but those in favour are not being very vocal. It is suggested that the matter is allowed to rest for a further two weeks, during which time the views of other groups will be forthcoming.

At the end of the second week, a representative of the Staff Nurses asks if a compromise would be acceptable. The suggestion is that the second staff nurse on each ward should be included in the rota, but not the nurse acting as Sister's deputy. Some careful thinking has to be done as this would affect the underlying principle of sharing night duty, especially among the more senior nursing staff.

5. *Describing the details and bringing the plan to effect*

Once agreement has been reached, there is a period required for setting the plan in action. Sisters are busy making out the rota for their own ward team. Those who are responsible for the allocation are ready to help since there may be individual difficulties.

It is recognised that the Ward Sister will in future be taking the responsibility for night duty cover, and that she will need to feel that she has the support and the security of the "pool" if she is unable to manage this.

Many of the difficulties are solved at ward level as the Sisters interpret the rota to the nursing team. Questions can be asked on the spot and be answered. The Night Sisters have their plans to make too, as they consider how the new scheme will affect the work of the hospital and the administration as a whole. The Home Wardens have had some reorganisation to do, and all have found that it is helpful if instructions which are given verbally are followed by clear concise written notices which give emphasis to the *main* points of change.

A short letter is sent to the Catering Officer and to the Domestic Superintendent reminding them of the date of the change. It has been agreed that the new rota will commence on all wards at the same time, rather than on a selected few.

6. *Evaluation of Success*

A trial period is set for this plan, giving a reasonable length of time for proper assessment. Notes are kept of problems as they arise. These include both favourable and unfavourable comments from patients and staff.

At the end of six months, the various groups meet again to share their views. Some difficulties have arisen which have already been solved, since it was felt that they were too urgent to leave until the final summing up. Advantages are weighed against disadvantages, keeping in mind the original objectives which justified the change.

CONCLUSION

If this example is examined carefully, the reader will realise that there are two essentials if a new scheme is to be introduced successfully. The first is the ability to adapt to different circumstances, and the second is the consciousness of the value of something new. This may mean that some people have to change their ideas, and this is not easy.

Sometimes in spite of being given considerable help, they are not able to do this, and it must therefore be accepted that there will be circumstances in which change cannot take place. When this happens, it is far better to recognise it and try to make the best of the situation which exists.

Senior Nurses must be prepared that once they embark on a change, they will probably produce the need for another. If an alteration is made when dressmaking, it is soon discovered that adjustments will be necessary in another part of the garment as well! People do not work in isolation; someone else is continually being influenced, either consciously or unconsciously. New thoughts must therefore be well-considered as, once they are let loose, they can spread like fire and, while this can act as a torch to new and better things, it can also burn up much that is of value and worth preserving.

SUGGESTION FOR FURTHER READING

World Health Organisation Technical Report No. 91. Expert Committee on Nursing. Third Report Nov. 1954 (Ch. 3). Published by W.H.O., Palais de Nations, Geneva.

SUGGESTIONS FOR FURTHER STUDY

MIDDLE MANAGEMENT

Describe the process by which a change could be made to the use of Central Sterile Supply throughout the hospital, which would maintain reliable and uniform procedures, acceptable to the medical and nursing staff, and also those responsible for the clinical instruction of nurses in training.

FIRST LEVEL MANAGEMENT

The following circumstances would appear to necessitate a change, either of policy or practice. Describe the procedure to bring the change into effect, in one of the situations.

1. A mishap occurs in the ward; a first year student nurse not

fully understanding her responsibilities, gives a diabetic patient who is not stabilized, a lunch from the ordinary menu. The Ward Sister is on holiday, and usually distributes all the diets herself.

2. It is a ruling of the hospital that all patients for admission from the Waiting List shall arrive at 10.0 a.m. in order that pre-operative investigations may take place. Owing to pressure in the ward, the beds are seldom ready for these patients until after midday.

3. A newly-qualified Staff Nurse is in charge of a Ward, and a patient complains that he has lost his dentures. He states that he left them in a mug in his locker while he went to the toilet. The Staff Nurse, not having met this situation before, arranges for him to see the hospital dentist with a view to obtaining a replacement. She takes no further action.

CHAPTER 4

IMPLEMENTATION OF POLICY

DELEGATION AND SUPERVISION

IF there is to be satisfactory management in any organisation, there must be lines of responsibility laid down and a structure which is established and recognised as being necessary for good work.

The Salmon Committee have shown in their Report[1] how this can be done within the framework of the nursing hierarchy. This Report stresses the fact that nurses in control at every level, including those at the "top" who co-ordinate the service, must be able to entrust duties and responsibilities to their colleagues. For many reasons senior nurses in the past, have not always found this easy. It is worthwhile considering why people sometimes find it hard to delegate, and the reasons why it is important to do so.

FAILING TO DELEGATE

In her Study of the Nursing Service of a General Hospital[2] Isobel Menzies states how nurses "bear the full, immediate and concentrated impact of stresses arising from patient care". She goes on to explain the reaction which occurs because of this situation and how "tasks are frequently forced upwards in the hierarchy so that all responsibility for their performance can be disclaimed". This is understandable if those in the team do not feel they are adequately prepared, or if there are not enough people of the necessary calibre who can assume responsibility; but sometimes those in charge do not delegate even when they have subordinates who are sufficiently able, and can be trusted.

Responsibility has been defined as "the ability and willingness to anticipate the results of one's actions, and in the light of the results—to act".[3] It appears that sometimes senior nurses interpret "being responsible" as being efficient in particular tasks, and do not consider the ability to make decisions and direct a situation as important as the performance of a series of individual duties. This state of affairs may have been aggravated by the present pattern of ward administration known as "job assignment", which will be discussed in a later chapter.

There are people who will not delegate because they feel that if they do so, they will lose prestige and authority. This is an unfortunate situation, because they miss the thrill of seeing their subordinates develop their skills and the satisfaction of knowing that that they helped them to become proficient. Perhaps they feel that, by holding on to all their tasks, they can prove that they are essential to the organisation: it is only natural for a person to want to feel needed. However, this situation can only lead to disaster, because those in authority become so overburdened that they are no longer able to retain the width of outlook which is essential for good management. There is no room to take on new responsibilities, and the result is lack of progress. Such pressure also produces symptoms of overwork and overstrain, and the consequent frustration is passed on to the rest of the team.

WHY DELEGATION IS NECESSARY

Mention has already been made of the satisfaction to be obtained from watching people develop confidence and ability. Delegation is part of the process of learning, and skills must be passed on so that, in time, others will be prepared for more important tasks. This is particularly necessary in a profession. Sometimes it is forgotten that the professional person is already committed, that there has been a deep conviction from the beginning that there is something worthwhile to be achieved. Therefore, if there is frustration and no recognition of this desire to help, the incentive which is inherent will disappear, and disillusionment will take its place.

Some people will be ambitious. This may not be a bad thing, but it is the motive behind it that matters. Aspiration to further responsibility can be either for the sake of prestige, or for the opportunity of greater service. It is right, therefore, that provision should be made for people to prove their ability, and that there should be recognition of those who work particularly hard and show special qualities.

RESPONSIBILITY WITH AUTHORITY

When an assignment or a duty has been delegated, it is of vital importance that the person who will carry it out, is given full authority to act in the way he or she thinks best. There can be few situations more frustrating than to be given a job to do, and then find that there are limits which confine the scope, or even worse, that someone else has been given the same task. There is an art in giving the necessary guidance and control without destroying a person's confidence. Over-criticism must be avoided, and at the same time standards must be maintained. Sometimes people appear to have failed in a particular assignment when, in fact, they have not been given adequate instructions in the first instance, or have failed to understand what is required of them. Clear directions must therefore be given initially, and then the person must be trusted.

Ideally, tasks should only be delegated which are known to be within the grasp of the individual who will be responsible. Sometimes it is necessary in special circumstances to delegate a more exacting duty. This can provide a stimulus and sense of achievement, and it is rewarding to see how people respond on such occasions, and gain encouragement. However, it must be remembered that greater vigilance will be required, and support must be readily available. Senior nurses should keep in mind that if they delegate a task to someone who has not had the requisite training, it is they who will stand responsible. This fact is not always recognised. It is especially relevant when considering the role of the nurse whose care of the patient requires much understanding of scientific equipment. This is a technical age, and it is essential that nurses give careful consideration to these matters.

SELECTING OTHER LEADERS

In order that administration can be effective, those in authority will need to have others working with them who can share the responsibility: people whom they can trust—and it must be a *mutual* trust. From this will spring the loyalty which is so essential, and the integrity without which no progress can be made. It is well-known that attitudes at all levels are usually a reflection of administrative relations higher up. If things are not "right", and seen to be so, among those who lead, there is little hope of contentment among the ranks.

Senior Nurse Administrators and Tutors will need to choose people to help them. It is sometimes tempting to appoint someone because their personal qualities are attractive, or because they have similar ideas. This is all right as far as it goes, but it is also necessary to consider the needs of the organisation as a whole. Will this person obtain the best from those for whom she will be responsible? Will she have an understanding of the problems, and sufficient experience and maturity to deal with them as they arise?

Many of the senior appointments will be made by a committee set up for the purpose. They, however, may need guidance because these are decisions which must be taken with the utmost care as they affect so many people. It is a forward step that outside assessors are now to be included for certain nursing posts,[4] but there is need for more research and inquiry into methods of selection and interviewing.

The Ward Sister also needs a colleague with whom to share some of her burden. The partnership which can exist between her and her staff nurse can be a most enjoyable experience for them both, and the Sister is wise who encourages a third year student who shows promise on her particular ward to return when she is qualified. Sometimes the nurse may hesitate because she lacks confidence in her ability, but this kind of stimulus may be just what she is wanting.

RELATIONS BETWEEN THOSE SHARING AUTHORITY

Loyalty and integrity have already been mentioned, and those who share responsibility and authority must believe that the same things matter, and work towards the same goal. This is not always easy when an experienced colleague holds personal views which conflict with those of the person at the head. However, outwardly there must be no differences. Any disagreement must be talked over in private. This is part of the sharing which, if it is based on mutual respect, will welcome participation in all things, in the sure knowledge that confidence will not be broken, and that what is discussed will always be directed towards the good of the whole. Frank opinions given with kindness and understanding as the underlying motives can help people to learn much about themselves. They must, however, be receptive.

There is one kind of discussion which is to be discouraged: namely talk about other colleagues who share similar responsibilities. Distrust and disharmony can be caused because it is thought that someone has a "private ear", or that personalities are being brought into the conversation. The nurse at the head must be impartial and absolutely fair in all situations. This will mean that sometimes it will be necessary to draw out a particular colleague who is reticent, and to hold back the more forceful one.

Finally, those to whom responsibility is delegated must be confident that, if things go wrong, they will have support from their leader. Mistakes will happen, and everyone has to learn, but these situations test the loyalty and integrity of the members of the staff. The Nurse-in-Charge must be able to give encouragement when colleagues become disheartened, and provide the wisdom which will show them how to avoid going wrong another time.

SUPERVISION

An attempt has been made to describe the teamwork which should exist among immediate colleagues. Having delegated responsibilities nurses will require an understanding of the art of supervision.

Much attention has been given to supervisory duties in the Industrial field, and an experiment which was undertaken at the Western Electric Company in Chicago, U.S.A. at the Hawthorne Plant illustrates certain points which are worth noting:

The Managers wanted to find out the effect which certain conditions of work had on employees and, particularly whether fatigue was a factor in the rate of production. Many experiments took place which will not be described in detail: more frequent rest-breaks were given, a shorter working week, and refreshments were allowed during the shifts. Production did go up, but it went up again when the group concerned returned to the old conditions. The reason for this was found to be the change in supervisor. He had come to them at the beginning of the experiment, but had remained when the girls returned to their former conditions. He had, however, been particularly interested in them because of what was going on, and had been able to enter wholeheartedly into their achievements and all that they were doing. As a special observer responsible to the research organisers, he enlisted their participation and co-operation in the experiment, so that they felt they were playing a part in the planning of their work, and were all the more prepared to make it successful.

There are several things which can be learnt from this. Firstly, that the response obtained from those who are working depends very largely on the amount they are allowed to share in the project, and on whether they feel that it really is their concern. Secondly, whilst the work is proceeding, the more it is made interesting with room for ingenuity and creative thought, the greater will be the accomplishment. Thirdly, encouragement and appreciation will stimulate the group and produce security.

ASSESSING PROGRESS

Good supervisors have a clear outline of what they expect from those in the team, and a definite routine for assessing progress. They may obtain their information by observations made at a specific time for that purpose as, for example, when an assessment takes place on the ward at the end of the student nurse's first year; or they may rely on daily contact. In the ward situation, some help will be obtained from the Staff Nurse who should be encouraged to give her opinion regarding the progress of the members of the nursing team. However, the Ward Sister will be wise to try to get to know the nurses individually and, if possible, find opportunities to work with them and see for herself how they approach patients and anticipate their needs.

The Senior Nurse Administrator or Tutor who is required to prepare reports on other members of staff will find it helpful to make notes from time to time to act as a guide when a final assessment has to be prepared. It is unsatisfactory to rely on memory, especially when large numbers of people are involved.

PREPARATION OF WRITTEN REPORTS

There are various ways of obtaining information about the progress of nurses in training,[5] and the value of written reports has been criticised on many accounts. It is easy to allow personal prejudice or preference to creep in so that opinion is biased, but if statements are written conscientiously and with an open mind they can provide useful information. It is most important that such reports are confidential to the person who is entitled to receive this information, and they should always be placed in an envelope marked "confidential", which is then sealed.[6]

There are different opinions concerning the presentation of these reports to the nurses themselves, so that they may learn of their progress. Whatever the practice, it is essential that students and pupils should know how they are getting on—the maxim that "no news is good news" is not compatible with good training methods.

REFERENCES

All that has been said about the writing of reports can equally be applied to the writing of references. This is not a matter which can be undertaken lightly, and the nurses must be prepared to spend considerable time and thought in order that what is written may be accurate, just, and helpful to the person who receives it. This is a heavy responsibility, and the Principal Nurse will be greatly assisted in her task if records are kept up to date and with care.

Sometimes it will be necessary to provide information concerning a member of staff who has not made a good contribution. In these circumstances it is important to state any points which are to her credit, but to remember that to give a false impression of a person's ability is a serious offence. Sometimes the very fact that some information is omitted can convey the situation to the recipient more forcefully.

It is important to read the request for a reference carefully, and to be sure that the specific questions which are asked about a candidate are answered. These questions will have been framed with a particular appointment in mind, and therefore the replies should greatly assist when selecting suitable applicants.

CONSTRUCTIVE CRITICISM

If work is not being done well, the supervisor must find out the reason. It may be that the task is beyond the capacity of the person who is undertaking it, or there may be overstrain and physical difficulties. The Senior Nurse must be on the alert for such problems so that steps can be taken to help before they reach major proportions.

There will be occasions, however, when members of the nursing team are not measuring up to what is expected of them, and correction of faulty technique, or guidance of some kind, will be required. Criticism must always be constructive. It is always possible to find some good point which can be commended at the same time. There is never any excuse for causing humiliation, and whatever has to be said must be to the nurse alone, and away from colleagues. When the matter has been put right, both the Nurse-in-Charge and the one who has been corrected should feel that it has been worthwhile.

It is necessary to follow up an occasion such as this, to make sure that the nurse has benefited, and understood what was wrong. She may require special encouragement for a time, and appreciation of any progress that is made will help her considerably.

ORIENTATION OF NEWCOMERS

However good the supervision or the delegation, both will fail unless an attempt is made to introduce the newcomer to the hospital by special training or instruction. There are certain facts that anyone who is new will wish to know:

1. The content of the job, and what is expected of her.
2. To whom she is responsible.
3. Her job in relation to that of others.
4. Conditions of service—salary, annual leave, etc.
5. Information concerning the hospital as a whole.

It is possible that a booklet giving details of the hospital will be available, but if not, arrangements should be made for the history and background to be given so that there is an understanding which can help the newcomer to feel she "belongs".

When people first arrive they are most receptive, so this is the time to organise a programme which will give a comprehensive picture of the work of the hospital, and provide an opportunity to make introductions to the other members of the staff. This is time-consuming, but most worthwhile, so long as this orientation is supervised by an experienced person, and not left to the last person to join the staff.

Some hospitals have introduced "documents" which describe the responsibilities and duties of the newcomer. If these are carefully compiled and kept up to date, they can be of great value.

At the beginning of this chapter reference was made to the importance of well-defined lines of responsibility: it is the duty of the Nurse-in-Charge to be sure that everyone knows to whom they may go when in difficulty, and to whom they are responsible. This is particularly important for the new member of staff, and can make all the difference to the speed with which she settles down and feels secure in strange surroundings.

REFERENCES

[1] Report of the Committee on the Senior Nursing Staff Structure. Ministry of Health and Scottish Home and Health Department.

[2] *The Functioning of Social Systems as a Defence against Anxiety.* A Report on a Study of the Nursing Service of a General Hospital, Isobel E. P. Menzies. Published by Tavistock Institute of Human Relations, 1961.

[3] *Personality and Problems of Adjustment,* Kimball Young, p. 422. Published by Kegan Paul, Trench, Tridner & Co. Ltd.

[4] Hospital Memorandum (66) 4.

[5] A Study of Student Nurses' Progress Reports—Interim Report— King Edward's Hospital Fund for London Hospital Centre, pp. 26-28.

[6] *Law Notes for Nurses,* S. R. Speller, LL.B., pp. 26-28. Published by the Royal College of Nursing and National Council for Nurses.

SUGGESTION FOR FURTHER READING

The Successful Supervisor in Government and Business, by W. R. Van Dersal. Published by Harper & Row, New York.

SUGGESTION FOR FURTHER STUDY

Supervision is essential to good management. Consider the leadership qualities which are required when taking the part of the supervisor in the hospital ward or department.

CHAPTER 5

IMPLEMENTATION OF POLICY

ORGANISATION FOR ACTION

IF there is to be organisation, there must be a framework, with different levels of responsibility. J. C. Mooney and A. C. Reiley, two Americans, describe this as the "Scalar Process". It has been referred to in this book as "lines of responsibility", but whatever it is called, it is proved that this process of delegation and supervision must be protracted through the whole enterprise in order that there may be effective action and results.

The larger and more complex the structure, the greater will be the need for co-ordination of all these processes, and the exercise of control to make sure that everyone is working towards the main objective. This is essential in order that individual interests do not conflict with the good of the whole.

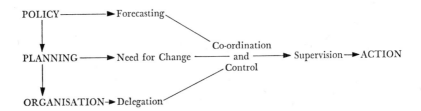

Within this framework, information and instructions must be able to travel freely from the top to the leaders at all levels. It is equally important that there should be free communication upwards. It must be possible for decisions to be made within the groups which make up the organisation since, if all matters have to travel to the top in the first place, not only is initiative strangled, but work grinds to a halt. There must be lateral links too, which bring the groups together, as their contribution will not be effective if they work in isolation.

This pattern can be likened to the building of a house. There is the architect who draws the plan (policy and planning) and the foremen who supervise on the building site (supervision). Groups of people work alongside one another—bricklayers, painters, plumbers, and electricians all have their brief, but it is in accordance with one design, and the collaboration of each group is necessary in order that the house may be habitable (co-ordination).

DIVISION OF RESPONSIBILITY

It has been said that five or six subordinates are the maximum for direct supervision.[1] The task of the manager, therefore, is to divide up the work of the organisation into viable and functional units which can each make their contribution, under the control of their own leaders. This can be done in two ways:

1. *Geographical Areas*

This is a familiar pattern for the delegation of work among Night Sisters in a hospital, where each will undertake the responsibility for a group of wards. It is becoming more common for the distribution of duties among Nurse Administrators, who instead of having a variety of responsibilities throughout the hospital, are able to concentrate on a specified clinical area. The advantages of this method are apparent, since it is possible to develop a keen interest in a smaller group and gain more understanding of their problems.

2. *Areas of Special Function*

It is an accepted fact that specialisation is inevitable if there is to be progress, and that people tend to know more and more about less and less! As there is advancement in the fields of medicine and surgery, so nursing, too, becomes more specialised. Over the last few years, units for the treatment of chronic renal failure, coronary care, and for intensive therapy have been developing rapidly, and it can be expected that further specialisation will follow. It can be of the greatest benefit to the patient if the nurses who care for them and supervise the wards in which they are nursed are experts in that particular field—the complexity of some of the work makes this essential.

Having accepted this, the Nurse Administrator has to understand more than ever the true meaning of delegation and of her part as a co-ordinator. She cannot expect to be conversant with the many developments in the clinical field, nor is this necessary if a firm reliance and trust is placed with the nursing heads of the various departments. Great unhappiness can be caused if those in authority try to "hold on" to the day-to-day management which should rightly be the province of the Nurse-in-Charge of a special ward or department. For example a member of staff may be appointed without any reference to this nurse, and yet she is often the only one who is familiar with the kind of work to be done, and will have a very good idea of the type of candidate who will best fill the post. There are several ward clerks in hospitals who were appointed to assist the ward sister without reference to her at the time of selection.

There are further problems which may arise from specialisation; namely the danger that this may segregate people into water-tight compartments, and that those in charge may rely too much on their own resources, ignoring the contribution which can be made by those around them. This can be overcome by good management, which helps nurses to realise their inter-dependence, and the necessity for sharing experiences. More will be said about this in the chapter on communications.

SELECTION OF PERSONNEL

Mention has already been made of the care with which selection of nurses who are to undertake positions of leadership should be carried out, but the choice of the right person for the job is important at all levels, and it is worthwhile considering some of the chief factors. Not everyone is a good judge of people, and selection of personnel is an exacting and difficult task. Sometimes mistakes are made because those making the decision are unsure themselves of the type of candidate required. This may be because there has been insufficient care in assessing the situation, or ignorance of the work involved. *It is important to have a clear written statement of the duties which are to be performed.* These three points can be helpful, if they are kept in mind:

1. The type of person to fill the post—personal and intellectual qualities—age—experience, etc.
2. The environment in which the work will be done.
3. The people with whom this person will accomplish the task.
                                                          (See Appendix A.)

The necessity for including other interested parties in the selection of new staff has been mentioned, and medical colleagues must not be forgotten, particularly when appointing or promoting nurses at Ward Sister level.

ALLOCATION OF DUTIES

When considering the allocation of duties to any group of people, it is important to look at each person's responsibilities in relation to the function of the whole. If this is not done, it is easy to overload certain members, or even to duplicate the work.

A good deal of emphasis has already been made on the choice of the right person, but it is not always possible to find exactly what is required. To what extent, therefore, should plans be modified and tasks adjusted to fit in with difficult personalities and those who are not quite up to the task? How far should those in authority go in accepting the wishes of individuals which do not fit in with the general plan? The answer is quite straightforward: on no account should be the principles of good organisation be laid aside to accommodate the idiosyncrasies of the few. In attempting to change one part of the plan to satisfy a personal need or fancy, it may be that the plan itself will disappear. This does not mean that the leader is inflexible—it is the fundamentals which must not change. In his book *Elements of Administration*,[2] Colonel Urwick describes this as the "inflexibility of a steel blade". The point can bend right down to the hilt, but when released it will spring back immediately into position. The vital factor is the sense of direction, and nothing should sway those in charge from following this, however difficult and however unpopular it may prove to be.

EXAMPLE

A Day Centre is to be set up for elderly patients in the district to provide diversional therapy and companionship. Someone then suggests that it might be possible to undertake clinical investigations and treatments for these patients as well. This could easily turn the Day Centre into a Day Hospital, with different staffing needs, and quite a different character—which would defeat the original objective.

The points which have been referred to in connection with the selection of staff need also to be kept in mind when allocating the work which is to be done. An example from the ward situation may help to illustrate this.

EXAMPLE

The Ward Sister when organising the nursing team will need to consider the type of people she has to do the job, the environment, and the kind of patients the nurses will be caring for. Supposing she is going to establish nursing of the patients by Group Assignment. It may be that a pattern of progressive care will be desirable, especially if there is a shortage of experienced nurses. Dividing the work according to the dependency of the patients has much to commend it, but Sister will need to remember her responsibilities for giving nurses in training the experience they require, and also the need for the patients to have continuity of care.

The physical construction of the ward will influence the grouping of patients, especially where there are side rooms, or part of the ward where observation may be more difficult.

In selecting the nursing teams, leaders will be appointed with sufficient support to enable them to delegate and provide the necessary help and supervision for those less experienced members. It will be necessary therefore to establish a balanced team so that the ward organisation may be smooth and satisfactory.

Finally, knowing the patients and their needs, Sister will want to make sure that those who most require help, whether of body or of mind, are able to receive it; and knowing the nurses, she will try to give them the opportunity to fulfil themselves in the tasks they undertake.

This example shows the many factors which need to be taken into consideration when organising the pattern of nursing care, and how essential it is that, in this case, the Ward Sister is completely conversant with the work which is to be done, and can tell who is the best person to do it.

JOB DESCRIPTIONS

There has been some reluctance in hospitals to write down what is required of those who make up the nursing team. This may be because nursing, dealing as it does with human beings, can never be "cut and dried", and it would be a tragedy if nurses were to confine themselves to a work list. On the other hand, there is a difference between the work schedule which is confined to the allocation of various duties, and the guidance which can help people to know which way they are going and what is expected of them. (See Appendix C.) Efficiency has been described as an aid to contentment, and if the organisation is to run smoothly it will be necessary to agree on certain procedures and issue instructions.

If the information is prepared in the form of guidance only, the essential points must be written down as otherwise the material becomes too complicated. There is an art in producing documents which are clear and concise, and yet sufficiently interesting to be readable. Student nurses when first entering a specialised unit such as a paediatric ward or operating theatre can be greatly helped if brief but relevant details are collected together about the work in that particular sphere. This can save senior staff from repeating instructions, and in some cases may avoid direct supervision. Such measures also help people to feel they belong and that they have a definite job to do.

If a ward is to be successfully administered, domestic staff will also require some guidance: clarification of the tasks to be done should not be confined to those actually nursing the patients. It could be said that the domestic staff schedules are the province of their Superintendent, but it is essential that they are discussed and agreed with the Ward Sister. A great deal of time can be lost by relief orderlies and domestic assistants who, when moving between wards, have to adapt themselves to other methods and routine.

The importance of having recognised nursing procedures is obvious, but there are other ways of improving organisation. Some hospitals have prepared reference books in which all administrative details may be found, such as the routine when an accident occurs to a patient or members of the staff. These are matters which are taught, but there are newcomers from other hospitals and less experienced people for whom this can be a valuable aide-memoire.

Economy of Time and Effort

There are occasions when a practice is perpetuated, or a job continued, not because it serves a useful function, but because somebody likes doing it, or thinks it is essential, or because by taking it away, they will lose prestige. There can be few appointments which have changed more in character than those of the British Matron over the past fifty years. From being the "housekeeper" as well as the person responsible for the patient's nursing care, she has in most instances handed over the duties of catering, domestic supervision and linen-room administration to other people, thus allowing time to concentrate on those responsibilities which require her professional knowledge and skill.

It is clear that if patients are to receive skilled nursing from those qualified to give it, serious thought must be given to the use of staff, and every effort must be made to concentrate available resources towards direct patient care. This means a critical and objective survey of the tasks which nurses perform, and a consideration in some instances of whether they need to be done at all. Nurses at all levels must be on the alert to challenge out-moded practices and performances which have lost their meaning and purpose. This takes courage and may necessitate self-examination, not only on the part of the nurse herself, but also among other members of the staff.

Organisation and Method (Work Study)

Work study is not a substitute for good management, but is identified as one of the "tools" of management. The first "motion study" was carried out by Frank Gilbreth in the nineteenth century whilst brick-laying in New England. Readers may refer to books which have been specially written on this subject for detailed information, and there are now short courses available which nurses may attend to help them to understand work study methods. However, it may be helpful to consider briefly the way in which these exercises are carried out, so that nurses in charge of departments may have them in mind when examining situations as they arise. The table opposite (from R. M. Currie's book on "Work Study") shows the procedure. This is the "critical examination sheet", and the starting point. Having acquired this information, accuracy must be checked, and then a summary prepared of what *should* be done. It is necessary to take into account other factors such as environment, working conditions, the output of energy, fatigue, and personal needs.

Sometimes resistance to work study is based on suspicion and possible fear of redundancy. Uneasiness may be caused by rumours spreading about the appearance of work study officers, and staff may attribute this to a criticism of their work.

If an investigation is to be undertaken by trained experts, the nursing staff should be given a detailed explanation of the object of the exercise, so that they welcome any recommendations that may come and are willing to implement them.

Reports on an investigation of this nature must never be in the form of a reproach, and suggestions must be constructive and aim at improving method and efficiency.

To be effective, work study should be a continuous process, and every improvement needs to be followed up. It is really no more than applied common sense, but the secret is that it is done objectively, and with fixed aims of producing order and efficiency in the best possible way.

CENTRALISATION

There has been much attention given to this over the past few years. Many of the services of the hospital have been centralised, with subsequent improvement in efficiency. There is still, however, much more that could be done—such as "topping-up" systems which will save the ordering of supplies and stores. It sometimes happens that a ward clerk is engaged to attend to these matters whereas, if supplies, maintenance and many other services were organised centrally, there could be a saving in labour and time. There have been Central Sterile Supply Departments started in small rooms with the minimum of equipment which have proved their worth. There may not be economic savings to show the Finance Officer, but nursing time can be saved, allowing the service to patients to be improved.

AUTOMATION

This is the age of the computer. Nurses should not be afraid to investigate the possibilities which they offer. It has been said that in ten years' time, the computer will be as useful to us mentally as the car is today physically. Already experiments are being made in their use for the allocation of student nurses for clinical ex-

DESCRIPTION OF ELEMENT

The Present Facts		Alternatives	Selected Alternative for Development
Purpose—WHAT is achieved?	IS IT NECESSARY? YES NO IF YES—WHY?	What ELSE could be done?	What?
Place—WHERE is it done?	WHY THERE?	Where ELSE could it be done?	Where?
Sequence—WHEN is it done?	WHY THEN?	When ELSE could it be done?	When?
Person—WHO does it?	WHY THAT PERSON?	Who ELSE could do it?	Who?
Means—HOW is it done?	WHY THAT WAY?	How ELSE could it be done?	How?

perience. It is too early to say what the results will be. It is known that there are high costs, and that the preparation of the programme is highly complicated. The nurse's part at the moment, is to keep an open mind, to read about the work that is being done, and to be prepared to accept the changes which may come. Welford in his article *Ergonomics of Automation* says this:

"Although automatic methods may reduce the immediate part played by human operators, they leave human beings in certain key positions in which the mental load upon them may be heavy, and the effects of their actions far-reaching. The human link in the system thus becomes more, and not less important than it was before."[3] Nurses must be prepared to provide that human link, and some will need to learn the art of programming.

When someone is trying to control a changing situation, they can only respond to those changes of which they are aware, and which form part of past knowledge. The computer, by collecting and analysing the data which it holds, can help to detect changes more readily and thus perform more efficiently. At the bedside, therefore, the computer will detect changes as they are happening, and give notice when abnormal conditions require the nurse's skilled attention without continuous personal supervision. To some, this may appear as a threat to the very personal service which the profession likes to give to patients, but the nurse will always be needed.

The monitor is already accepted, and surgical operations can be observed in another part of the building by means of television. The impact of modern scientific inventions can be frightening, and there may be some difficult problems to be solved in the future. Earlier in this book the question of retaining the necessary values in a time of change was discussed—nurses have a responsibility to see that patients do not lose privacy, nor their identity as people, with very individual needs. I. F. Detwiller describes this when writing about "Automation in the Hospital", and says that "the patient cannot be allowed to become too automated because of the part direct human care plays in his treatment and recovery. Somewhere between an extreme degree of automation and today's treatment patterns, lies the probable answer, and we will have to find the right point of compromise."[4]

OFFICE AIDS

Owing to the shortage of trained typists, it is becoming essential for nurses in administrative appointments to know how to use dictating machines. Once the technique is mastered it can be a valuable time-saver.

There are other mechanical aids for the modern office which will not be enumerated here, but most nurses will be familiar with such things as the "Graphdex" Board for listing names and enabling a picture of the staff allocation to be obtained at a glance. These boards are of no value unless they are kept up to date, and they should be used only as an aid to memory, and not as a substitute for good planning.

STATISTICS

Nurses are sometimes frightened of statistics, and feel they have no place in the world in which they function. This is not true, and shows a lack of awareness of the value of statistics in helping to make decisions for the future, by having a picture of the past.

Statistics of the numbers of nurses who are sick, and the incidents in the different grades, can give valuable information. Trends can be watched in this way, so that action can be taken as necessary. It is sometimes useful to plot this information on a graph if statistics over a long period are required for discussion at a committee. Numbers of applications for appointments on the staff can be treated in the same way, and also details of wastage. It is far better to have these figures maintained in an orderly way than to be caught unawares, and then to have to spend hours—or even days—making calculations. It is also more efficient.

OFFICE MANAGEMENT

No chapter on organisation would be complete without reference to the importance of this subject. In all the new District Hospitals which are being planned, offices for the various senior members of staff are included. There is no doubt that the tendency to increase paper work is to be discouraged, but there are certain advantages in having information collected in one place. The "office" should be a vantage point from which can flow productive material, not a storehouse which is stagnant. It provides a base for personnel, from which they may obtain information, not a retreat from the active scene.

Much of the material which is described will only be applicable to the nurse at middle or top management levels, but there is no harm in considering the principles, some of which can equally apply to the management of the office in the ward or department.

RECORDS AND WRITTEN NOTES

Some people rely on memory—but the manager in any organisation large or small, cannot give attention to all the demands which will be made on him, and at the same time keep information in his head. There is also the possibility that he or she will not be present when that information is required, or may have moved to another appointment. This is sometimes forgotten when it is a question of recording day-to-day events, and incidents which refer to personnel. In a hospital, a nurse may come with a difficulty and obtain advice. She goes away satisfied, but returns some months later with further problems in relation to the original. If no note has been made of the conversation on the first occasion it can be very difficult to pick up the threads, or even to remember what advice was given.

The official records concerning members of the staff are of vital importance, and cannot be treated lightly. This is a task which should be delegated, and done by clerical staff. However, it is essential that whoever is responsible is fully aware of the need to keep the contents in the strictest confidence, and always to have the records under lock and key. Entries must be made on the day on which an event takes place, be it sickness or a move to another department, since a faulty entry may have far-reaching effects. Legibility is also important, and mistakes have been known to occur in calculating dates because they have been so badly written. It is probably better that this information is typed.

Records need to be filed, and it is not proposed to discuss the different methods which are available. A visit to the Hospital Records Officer can be helpful, and most of the leading firms are only too pleased to send a representative to give advice. It is sufficient to emphasise that nurses should know the necessity for orderly filing, the dangers of mis-filing, and be able to keep material which is in their hands in confidence and security.

STANDARDISATION

The organisation of any office will be most efficient if there is some form of standardisation. This refers to records of all kinds. The information required should be kept to the minimum, and the presentation as simple as possible. The form of work study which has been described, can be applied to great advantage when dealing with "office work" in all situations.

OFFICE ROUTINE

There will be some nurses in positions of responsibility, who will be fortunate in having the assistance of others in dealing with the work which comes into the office. Indeed, it is time that nurses were more vocal in asking for sufficient help, so that experienced professional men and women do not waste their time attending to clerical duties.

A personal secretary can make all the difference to the busy life of senior nursing staff, and mutual trust will enable a great deal of work to be delegated with confidence. The Secretary may need to be helped and trained in the first instance, and it is worth spending time on this, and explaining the technical and specialised aspects of the job. She needs to have full knowledge of her employer's movements in order to deal with enquiries and telephone calls—there is nothing more frustrating than to find that the person who is wanted has disappeared without giving any indication of her whereabouts. The Secretary can draw attention to matters which are urgent, and can be invaluable when she discovers and rectifies a slip or oversight. Choice of staff in any administrative department is of great importance, since they set the tone, and give the first impressions in many situations. Not the least of these is the impact of the telephone. The response which a caller receives has a great influence on his idea of the hospital, and a bored and disinterested reply can be most frustrating, particularly when the caller is wanting help or is anxious. Although the clerical staff are employed by the lay administration, it is essential that nurses for whom they work should have an opportunity to take part in their appointment.

CORRESPONDENCE

On the whole, experienced nurses, however good they may be at their own work, are not so efficient when they have to perform duties such as dictation, which are commonplace in the life of most people in senior positions. This may be because in the past sufficient emphasis has not been laid on the need for nurses to be articulate. However, this should improve with modern nursing education, which encourages nurses to put thoughts and ideas forward for discussion.

Correspondence should be dealt with as early in the day as possible. It is easy to let other demands have priority, but very unfair to those who have to produce work by a given time. Prompt replies can make all the difference to the reaction of the recipient. Waiting two or three days for a reply gives a bad impression, and may even mean that the writer may lose interest in an application. It is a courtesy to acknowledge that the letter has been received, even if the answer is not readily available, and to indicate that a further reply will follow as soon as possible.

The manner in which a letter is written can also have considerable influence on the recipient. Formal acknowledgements of gifts or donations may appear to be satisfactory, but a personal letter which shows a warmth of appreciation and gives some indication of the pleasure that has been given, will mean much more. It is worthwhile taking this extra trouble.

In the same way that people should be treated as individuals worthy of personal attention, so also their correspondence deserves this respect. Casual and disinterested letters have no place in any administrative department which has a humanitarian leadership. It may be that the Nurse Administrator will have to train and teach those who are handling correspondence, especially if they have been brought up in a commercial firm, and are used to "business" jargon and formality. Much can be learnt by example.

FINANCIAL CONSIDERATIONS

1. Estimates

It is a sad reflection on the profession, that nurses often do not bother to find out where the money comes from which pays, not only for their own salaries, but for the equipment and the supplies which they use each day. Any Finance Officer will be only too pleased to explain these matters if he is asked, and since this money belongs to the tax-payer, nurses should take an interest. It is necessary for estimates of expenditure to be submitted to the Ministry of Health in order that the budget for the coming financial year may be arranged. Senior nurses at ward and departmental level are therefore asked every twelve months to indicate the equipment and furniture that they anticipate they will require. It is a good plan to keep a note during the year of items which are wearing out, or of a new commodity which would be beneficial, so that this information is at hand when needed. There is a skill in submitting these estimates so that the right priorities are forthcoming. It is well known that there is a limit to the amount of money, and if a request cannot be granted, a record can be made so that it can be brought forward another time. This is a form of "good housekeeping", and something which should not be neglected.

2. Establishments

Managers who are controlling a number of people on the staff of any organisation, should know their "establishment" or the number that should be in post at any given time. This includes a knowledge of full-time and part-time members. Nurse Administrators should be familiar with these facts, since there are financial implications. These must be known and understood in order to keep within the necessary financial limit. Changes need to be notified to the finance department, and a careful record kept of any variation in grade or number.

3. Departmental Costing

This subject is being included, at the risk of readers thinking that the narrative is becoming somewhat technical, because it is one that cannot be ignored. Nor is it right that nurses should dissociate themselves from a personal responsibility for the financial expenditure in the ward or department in which they work.

Uniform Costing was introduced into the Hospital Service in

1957, in an attempt to make a comparison between the actual amount of money absorbed by a department, and the estimate of need shown in the Budget. This system had been used in Industry as a means of improving efficiency, but the difficulty in hospitals was to measure "productivity"—how could the quality of service be estimated, since the amount of work done would not necessarily give an indication?

Before 1957, with the introduction of the National Health Service, the Ministry of Health Interim Costing Scheme asked for expenditure to be shown under various headings, drugs, salaries, etc. However, following an experiment by the Nuffield Provincial Hospitals Trust and the King Edward's Hospital Fund for London, it was decided to introduce a "cost unit" which would be a unit of measurement which could be applied in each department; for example, in the X-Ray department a Barium Meal would be 8 units. In this way the number of units used in each department could be estimated. It was felt that this system would enable a watch to be kept on the expenditure of individual departments, and provide a means of comparison not only within a particular hospital, but between hospitals. This in turn, would assist the distribution of available funds, and also help to keep down costs within reasonable limits.

It is necessary that this is known and understood, in order that those responsible for wards and departments can help their staff to be "cost conscious" and make a personal contribution to controlling excessive expenditure. There might be a few surprises and an economy drive if some inquiries were made about the cost of certain equipment and supplies. It might even be worth introducing a little healthy competition between departments to see who could maintain standards and still reduce costs.

Departmental costing can provide another useful function, in that it can highlight where there is under-spending, so that deficiencies can be remedied.

Many aspects of organisation have been studied which show how much attention has to be paid to this subject if plans and policy are to be implemented. There is not only the importance of having the right people in the right job, but the necessity to make sure they know what to do, and how to do it. Finally, they must feel they are an essential part of the organisation, working with colleagues towards a common objective.

REFERENCES

[1] *Reality of Management*, Rosemary Stewart, p. 30. Heinemann, London.

[2] *Elements of Administration*, L. Urwick, p. 30. Sir Isaac Pitman & Sons Ltd.

[3] *Ergonomics of Automation*, A. T. Welford. Problems of Progress in Industry No. 8. Department of Scientific and Industrial Research, published by H.M.S.O.

[4] "Automation in the Hospital," L. F. Detwiller, *Canadian Hospital*, Vol. 41, May 1964.

SUGGESTIONS FOR FURTHER READING

Work Study, by R. M. Currie. Published by Sir Isaac Pitman & Sons Ltd.

The Art of Administration (Ch. XV), by A. Leslie Banks and J. Hislop. Published by University Tutorial Press Ltd., London.

PART TWO

THE ART OF COMMUNICATION

Human growth is . . . the development of the capacity for communication. We learn to observe the world and people around us; to react to them and to attract their attention. We interpret, evaluate, and select the signals pressing in upon us from all sides.

Dr Magda Kelber—I.C.N. Congress, 1965

CHAPTER 6

COMMUNICATION SKILLS

DEVELOPMENTS of modern science have increased the populations within hospitals, and if the activity of twenty years ago is compared with that of the present day, it is obvious that skill in communication must be developed if people are to live in harmony and work effectively with one another. There has been some delay in realising this, but recently there have been several publications which have drawn attention to a failure in communication within the hospital. The Ministry of Health Circular "Communication between Doctors, Nurses and Patients"[1] made some suggestions, as did Ann Cartwright in her book *Human Relations and Hospital Care*.[2] In the *British Hospital Journal and Social Service Review*[3] an account is given of an appreciation course in "Hospital Internal Communications" attended by senior administrators, doctors and nurses sponsored by the Hospital Centre of the King Edward's Hospital Fund for London. It will be interesting to follow the work of Professor Revan's team on this subject.

The spotlight has indeed turned upon the hospital world, but there is much that can be done if people are prepared to take the trouble and accept the fact that communications are a problem. They can try to find out why this is so, and how the difficulties can be overcome.

It is a useful exercise for a member of the staff to sit down with a pencil and paper and write down all the names of the different people with whom they associate within a given time. The Staff Nurse might have a list something like this at the end of the morning:

Patients	Dietitian
Nurses	Domestic Supervisor
Domestic Staff	Relatives
Doctors	Pathology Technician
Physiotherapist	Hospital Plumber
Radiographer	Assistant Matron
Clinical Instructor	Hospital Porter
C.S.S.D. Staff	Telephone Operator.

The Principal Tutor and Matron would probably have lists which were equally varied, and so would the Hospital Secretary. Nurses expect to be in touch with all kinds of people, it is therefore worth considering what this requires of them, and the skill which must be developed if communications are to be effective.

THE TWO-WAY PROCESS

As soon as two people meet there is an impact—some kind of response. When they communicate there must also be active participation on *both* sides. This is true whether the communications are horizontal, between people working at the same level, or vertical, between the leaders of an organisation and those doing the job.

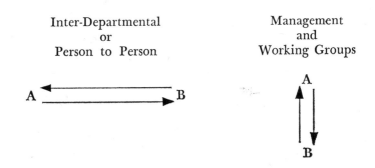

Inter-Departmental
or
Person to Person

Management
and
Working Groups

However brief this encounter is, some kind of relationship is made. However, this can be so weak that neither party benefits in any way, and the communication is sterile. A person who does not wish to become involved can keep at a distance, and make it impossible to produce what has been called "rapport". It is described as "the particular way in which we perceive and relate to our fellow human beings; it is composed of a cluster of inter-related thoughts and feelings".[4]

Good communications, therefore, depend greatly on the attitudes of the people who are in touch with one another, but are also influenced by many other factors. Verbal skill is necessary, and this requires clear thinking. Written communications need equal care. Sometimes it is under-estimated to how great an extent people convey their thoughts and feelings by their expression and where patients are concerned, by their touch.

VERBAL COMMUNICATION

During the course of conversation, the speaker is attempting to convey in words the thoughts which are in his mind. If these thoughts are confused, so will be the sentences which are spoken.

It is especially important, when an instruction is to be given, that the content is carefully considered beforehand or it will not convince the hearer or convey the desired message. If there is to be a difficult interview, it is wise to make a few notes beforehand so that the trend of thought can be built up logically.

CHOICE OF WORDS

However good the preparation, information will not be received unless it is presented in such a way that the recipient can understand. The simpler the language the better it will be understood, and great harm can be done by using technical jargon, and referring to subjects by initials which have no significance to those who are listening.

Pronunciation is important, and the speaker has to learn to be articulate. Often people do not understand because of the speed with which information is given, and sometimes because it is delivered in a monotonous voice which fails to give emphasis to points which should be remembered.

Generalities can be misleading, and the person who says "he would like to get the business done as soon as possible" is not going to obtain much response unless it is known of what the "business" consists.

Pitfalls arise when the words which the speaker is using mean something different to the listener. For example, someone may say "This work is not up to standard!" The person who is being approached may think that this means that it is below the standard of his usual work, whereas it was intended that he should understand that it was below the standard of the group as a whole. This is an instance of "lazy thinking" and the speaker should have been more specific. Sometimes the wrong interpretation may be made because just one word has a different significance. It must be remembered that for five hundred words which are used in the English Language, there are fourteen thousand possible meanings listed in the Oxford Dictionary. It is not surprising that mistakes can easily be made. Misunderstandings can be reduced to a minimum however, if trouble is taken to consider, not only the content of what is being said, but the person who is being addressed. This is particularly important in view of the fact that, in hospital, many people come from other countries and may have difficulty in understanding nurses who are talking to them.

THE LISTENER

No conversation or interview will bear fruit unless there is a willingness to listen. The person who is not giving his whole attention will not be able to comprehend what is being said. Concentration and effort are required, and the listener should participate by making comments which confirm that he is following the course of the dialogue. Asking questions which have a bearing on the subject will help to reassure his companion that he is being understood.

Having considered the part of the speaker and the listener, it may be useful to examine some of the barriers which make communication difficult and prevent people from being understood, and from getting into touch with one another.

1. *Failure to Make Time and Opportunity*

"Everyone was so busy, I did not like to bother them!" It is very sad when this is said, because it means that either some people are too preoccupied with the daily round, or their priorities are not right. It is particularly important that nurses in positions of responsibility should make themselves accessible to those they lead. Often it is just the knowledge that advice and help are readily available that keeps the group from unnecessarily worrying those in authority. It also means that problems are solved before they reach undue proportions. In his biography of Sir Alexander Fleming, André Maurois writes, "No matter what the work he was doing, a colleague had only to knock at his door, which always stood wide open, for him to say at once: 'Yes, come along in!' and to give his full attention to the tale of difficulty or discovery. One of his most precious qualities was this ability to detach his mind in a split second from what had been occupying it, and to go straight to the heart of the new problem. . . . A few minutes later there would be another knock at the door, and another young man would immediately receive the same attention."[5]

Note the word "same"; it is not always easy to appear relaxed and ready to give time in the midst of a busy day, especially when problems are particularly pressing. It means so much, however, to those who are seeking help, if they are greeted with courtesy, and made to feel that they are welcome.

2. *Uncongenial Atmosphere*

Some people are more sensitive to atmosphere than others but the attitude with which they are received will make all the difference to the success of an interview. On this may even depend whether the problem is voiced at all. It is not unknown for someone to go away after an interview without raising the subject, because they sensed "it was not the right day".

If the problem has been a worrying one, the person requiring help may be diffident and unsure of herself. She will need encouragement if she is to come to the point. Sometimes it is helpful to refer to another subject in the first place and then lead the conversation into the right channel. If she is able to feel a certain warmth in her reception she will be able to talk more readily, but she will be on the look-out for reactions, and any indication that she is not obtaining the undivided attention of her listener. Fidgeting with material on the desk can be most distracting, and so can interruptions by the telephone. Privacy is essential, and it is easier if the chair is placed to the side of the person conducting the interview and not opposite. This makes conversation less formal, and it is easier to disregard outward symbols of authority which may get in the way.

Mention has already been made of the parts which facial expression and tone of voice play in communication. It is also worth remembering that what is conveyed by touch can sometimes be more expressive of sympathy and understanding than words.

3. *Personal Idiosyncrasies and Prejudices*

Sometimes a barrier to good communication occurs when a person has preconceived ideas about another, so that when there is discussion free exchange of ideas is not possible. It may be that one member of the group insists on pressing her point regardless of the opinions of others, and is not open to suggestion. It is a sign of maturity to be prepared to accept the other person's point of view, and also to acknowledge the worth and uniqueness of each individual.

Sometimes it is possible to inhibit conversation by a tendency to over-criticise, and people are afraid to put forward their views. Fear can be one of the greatest hindrances. The person who "says what she thinks" will also produce fear, since lack of consideration for the feelings of others can often be humiliating and cruel. One of the essentials to the success of any interview, is that it produces confidence and does not destroy it. Talking down to people is never justified.

The importance of attitude cannot therefore be underestimated, for this provides the foundation of mutual trust. It means taking the trouble to see people as they are, and as they appear at the *particular moment*. They will not always be their normal selves, especially when under stress or strain. Those in positions of leadership should be ready to observe this, and to remember that there are some emotions which speak for themselves.

4. *Impatience*

Apart from the discourtesy, interruption of another person's conversation can be very upsetting. It is also wrong to bring the discussion to a premature close, since this may mean that a vital part of the discourse is never brought into the open. Contradiction at frequent intervals can also impede a conversation. This all sounds so obvious, but it is important to learn to control any tendency to break in and upset the other person's train of thought. It is also necessary to control emotion. The person who has come for help may be angry, and because of this approach it is easy to be roused as well. This will only make matters worse, and it is better to try to find out why there is anger or antagonism, since there may be a far deeper meaning behind this than appears on the surface. "Something has upset you—can I help?" may unlock the door and reveal what is being held within.

With these points in mind, it may be useful to consider the communications which should exist between the nurse and the patient.

EXAMPLE

Patients have to make considerable adjustments when they come to hospital. This is admirably described in an article "Communication—Some Psychological Aspects of the Nurse-Patient Relationship"[6] which appeared in the Nursing Press, and which all nurses would do well to read. The patient may be wondering who all these people are who administer to him, how will he know what to do, and what is going to happen to him? The activities which go on around him may fill him with foreboding, and will sometimes be misinterpreted. He may be embarrassed at finding himself in an open ward, and there will be unfamiliar sounds as well as unfamiliar surroundings. On top of all this he has his own trouble to contend with—pain and discomfort, anxiety for his own future and possibly for that of the family as well. His illness may have been in existence for some time, and the capacity for enduring pain and meeting new demands is consequently diminished. An illness is a breakdown of the human being's capacity to fight disease, and more than just the physical defences may have been broken down. The nurse's task is to help to build up these defences, so that ultimately the patient is able to control the situation himself.

Here then is an opportunity to create a rapport which will overcome two of the barriers to communication—fear, and a potentially uncongenial atmosphere that is strange and holds the possibility of pain and discomfort.

There is a hospital in America which has tried to meet this opportunity, by obtaining permission from the Consultant for the new patient to go to the dining-room with the nurse who will be looking after him for his first evening meal. The idea is that this patient will get to know the nurse and the other people in the ward, and conversation will take place in an informal atmosphere. This is an interesting experiment, but there are few who will unburden themselves in public, and what the patient needs from the nurse is her time and attention in privacy. "Am I allowed to ask?" may be a question in the patient's mind. Talking to him alone, the nurse can anticipate the things which he will want to know, and establish a relationship which makes communication possible and does away with fear.

Finally, there will be the need to preserve the dignity of the patient. We are all different, in temperament, age, race, creed and colour; self and mutual respect must be preserved at all costs. Expressions such as "Dad", "Dear" and "Grandma" have no place, and everyone is entitled to his own name, used as the nurse herself would wish if one of her own relatives were in the same position. It is also important that the patients see this same respect among the nursing team. Christian names and the casual use of "Staff"— which is meaningless—cannot help but diminish the patient's regard for the professionalism and efficiency of those who are looking after him.

Of necessity, very personal information may be required of patients from time to time. Such questions may cause embarrassment if asked in an impersonal way, and in this situation too, the attitude of the nurse can make all the difference.

It is worth noting that, quite unintentionally, nurses may put physical barriers between themselves and the patients or relatives. Sometimes it is argued "but the relatives never complained, and I was sitting in the office!" The nurse has not realised that even the "office" is a barrier. Perhaps Sister or Staff Nurse were having a conversation with a doctor, and it was thought that they should not be disturbed. This is the occasion when nurses need to go out into the ward or department and introduce themselves (name badges are only an aid, and not a substitute for introductions) and make it easy for people to talk to them. This takes time, and means extra effort, but it pays dividends.

In summing up these thoughts on communications with patients and their relatives, it would not be right to ignore the adjustment which has to be made by the nurse herself. The nurse too may be in a strange environment, and may even be afraid. Those in charge need to give thought to this, particularly with regard to the student and pupil nurses in training, remembering that they must have support if they in their turn are to help their patients. Perhaps example is the greatest assistance in these circumstances, coupled with a deep understanding of what it all means. Some of the emotional and trying situations which take place day by day in every hospital can be eased when those in authority will take the trouble to come to the level of nurse as well as patient, and say "Come, let us go along and face this one together!"

TRANSMITTING INFORMATION

At every turn of events, the nurse-in-charge should say to herself "who needs to know?" Occasionally people do not want to part with information because they feel that it adds to their prestige if they are the only ones who know. Such sentiments have no place when the giving of full and accurate details may influence the care of patients and the well-being of the organisation as a whole. It is of course necessary to consider what should not be discussed, since nurses are entrusted with much that is confidential, but it is essential to discriminate and to ensure that senior colleagues, in particular, have the information they require to make the right decisions and implement them. If they are ignored they will become insecure, and few things can upset good relations more easily than this.

EXAMPLE

Plans are made for closing wards for annual cleaning. The information will need to be conveyed to Ward Sisters, the Medical Staff, the Domestic Superintendent, and other Heads of Departments. It will also be required by those responsible for nurse allocation and nurse teaching. It may be that the student nurses on the Introductory Course are undertaking a series of ward visits arranged by the Tutors, and it can be very upsetting to find that plans have to be suddenly changed because a particular ward of patients is moving or closing.

Distorted or Inaccurate Information. Where there is faulty administration, and communications fail, there is a tendency to rely upon the "grapevine." This means, of course, that what is passed on is often incorrect or, because all the facts are not available, the gaps are filled by what people think or imagine is right. Unfortunately it is also true that if people are not sure what is happening they tend to think the worst. The situation is reminiscent of the game played by children when, sitting in a circle, a sentence is whispered to one of the party, and then in succession around the group. Great hilarity is caused when the last person says out loud what he has heard—it never resembles the original sentence. In adult life, misinterpreted information is not often hilarious; instead it causes harm to individuals, and maybe to the whole organisation. Relying on rumours or what has been overheard can be very dangerous.

Patterns and Channels of Communication. Making sure that the correct information reaches the right person at a suitable time is the essence of good management. Some communications will need to be in the form of a command. The situation may be tense or urgent, and a certain discipline is required to prevent serious mistakes. Nurses need to be helped to understand such circumstances, and to know that obedience at that time is vital, but that opportunity will be found to explain the details when the emergency is past.

There will be other occasions when, although there is no urgency, it may be wise to postpone the giving of information. Conveying a message when someone is distressed, or overburdened will sometimes mean that it is not absorbed or understood. It may also be necessary to allow time for people to get used to an idea when discussing the implementation of change (see chapter 3), but where the professional relationship is good, persuasion will be possible.

Noticeboards. These should never be relied upon as the sole means of giving instruction or information. If noticeboards are used they must be kept up to date, or people will pass them by because they have seen all the notices before, and in this way they miss the odd bit of news. It is helpful if a section can be reserved for fresh items, and a label added to draw attention to the latest one to be posted. The placing of the board is important, and it is useful to make one person responsible for its upkeep.

Committees and Conferences. The good manager will see that there are established committees which form a stable link with the various groups in the organisation. In hospital, these will vary and it is not proposed to make a list of those which may be found. However, Nurse Administrators will need to examine these links from time to time to make sure they serve the function for which they were intended, and that they are active, useful, and democratic in their outlook. Is the Nurse's Representative Council truly representative? Is the State Enrolled Nurse given her rightful place and an opportunity to bring forward her views from the wealth of experience which the more mature member possesses? Is the Student Nurse, who is taught to observe, think, and discuss, able to feel free to make her contribution; and is there a good line of communication from the representatives back to the groups concerned? These are all vital questions which must be asked over and over again, so that the pattern may be revised in the light of a changing situation.

The informal conferences which take place between professional groups are of the utmost value. Any occasion which brings together people who have the same goals, will be useful. Nurses in the psychiatric field have much to teach their colleagues about group discussion at ward level, and time spent in this way can often save confusion and misunderstanding.

There will also be formal committees which the Senior Nurse Administrator will need to attend. She should bring with her nurses at the head of any special departments whose particular fields are on the agenda. This is also important if several hospitals are represented in a Group, so that the Nurse-in-Charge of each particular area is able to speak from her knowledge of the situation.

Committees are formed to obtain a collective opinion, not to provide an escape for senior officers who do not want to make a decision. It is important that they should be business-like, for the people who attend are usually busy people with little time to spare. They are also some of the most "expensive members," earning professional salaries. The meeting should be properly convened, and have clear terms of reference. The agenda and all other relevant matter should be sent in good time—this preparation for a committee is important. Sometimes people fail to make their point because they have not studied the facts, or taken the trouble to think about the course of action they should take. Picking up the papers at the last minute and hurriedly making for the committee room can spell disaster.

There are plenty of reference books to which the reader may turn to understand the procedure which is accepted in this country for the conduct of committees, and every nurse should be familiar with this so that she is not afraid to take her part if her presence is requested. Such occasions should be welcomed as they provide an opportunity to make an active contribution to the work of the hospital. Certain types of members however often fail to play a useful part: the over-enthusiastic ones who prevent others from putting their point of view, the chatterers who keep up an undertone of disagreement, those who fail to keep to the point, and those who say nothing at all, but hold a post-mortem afterwards.

WRITTEN COMMUNICATIONS

A chapter on the art of communication would not be complete without some reference to the importance of what is written. Reference has already been made to correspondence, and much that has been said about verbal skills can be applied to written information. This must be clear, concise, and accurate. A long sentence will be fully understood by a smaller number of readers than a short one.

If possible, it is wise to give advanced warning of a written instruction, so that the gist of what is required is already understood and acceptable. In the same way, it helps if people are told beforehand if they are going to be asked to fill in a particular form, or provide certain statistics. A sudden demand made to an already harassed member of the staff can be very upsetting, and what seems quite a simple matter may require considerable effort when it is in addition to the daily load. It is also right that the recipient should know why the information is required. This can make all the difference to the amount of co-operation which is given, and the speed with which the details are produced.

There are occasions when written communications are out of place—for instance, if a difficulty arises between two heads of departments because one of them has failed to provide certain equipment. Sitting down to write an official complaint in the heat of the moment is not going to put matters right. A personal visit, made when both sides have had time to clarify the situation, may bring together people who hitherto had not realised the impact which their own department had upon the other. It is good to remember that the best administration is done on foot.

Written Reports. The Ward Sister will be mainly concerned with the writing of daily reports about the patients. She may, however, be called upon to make statements concerning an accident which has occurred, or to describe a particular event which took place, in a case of litigation. It is therefore important that all nurses learn how to express themselves, and how to present their material in an orderly fashion. Senior nurses should be prepared to help those who are less experienced, since much may depend on these reports.

It is a good plan to make headings in the first place, and then to arrange the detailed information inside the overall pattern. A Report in preparation for a Committee will be found in Appendix B and, although this kind of report-writing will mainly fall within the province of the Senior Nurse Administrator, the outline can be used for simpler presentations at ward level.

It can be seen from the points which have been discussed, that successful communications depend largely on the ability and willingness of the leaders to study the ways in which people are in touch with one another, and how they receive and transmit information. The social skills cannot be separated from the importance of attitudes and of the environment. If there are free channels of communication, people will feel that they matter, and this feeling is the foundation on which good relationships throughout the organisation can be built. In the following chapters this aspect will be considered, and also how these principles can be applied to relationships beyond the hospital.

REFERENCES

[1] *Communication between Doctors, Nurses and Patients, an aspect of Human Relations in the Hospital Service.* Ministry of Health Joint Sub-Committee, S.N.A.C., Central Health Services Council, H.M.S.O.

[2] *Human Relations and Hospital Care,* Ann Cartwright. Routledge and Kegan Paul, 1964.

[3] "Hospital Internal Communications", *British Hospital Journal and Social Service Review,* 20.8.65 snf 21.1.66.

[4] "What do we mean by Rapport?" J. Travelbee. *American Journal of Nursing,* February 1963.

[5] *The Life of Sir Alexander Fleming* by André Maurois, translated by Gerard Hopkins.

[6] "Communication—Some Psychological Aspects of the Nurse-Patient Relationship," R. Hetherington, B.Sc., Ph.D., *Nursing Times,* 18.12.64.

SUGGESTIONS FOR FURTHER READING

The Patient's Attitude to Nursing Care, Anne McGhee, Chapters 7 and 10. Published by E. & S. Livingstone Ltd., London.

"No Time for Silence" by Eleanor M. Sykes—*American Journal of Nursing,* May 1966, page 1040.

"The Art of Interviewing (No. 1)" by May Slack, H.V. Cert., *Nursing Times,* 21.1.66, page 83.

Nurse and Patient—the Influence of Human Relationships, Genevieve Burton. Published by Tavistock.

Committee Procedure, Kay Gilmour, F.R.G.S. Published by Methuen, 1950.

SUGGESTIONS FOR FURTHER STUDY

1. Statement for discussion: It has been said that "The stability of an organisation is dependent on the information which is received, and how it is received." Alvin C. Leyton.

2. Consider from past experience, occasions on which communications have failed, either between Senior Nurse Administrator and the Ward or Departmental Nursing Staff, or between the nursing team at this level and those responsible for the Nursing Administration. Why did this happen? How could it have been avoided?

CHAPTER 7

COMMUNICATIONS AND GOOD RELATIONS

THOSE who have studied the behaviour of groups of people, tell us that they have distinctive characteristics. This can be said to be true of the various groups within a hospital. Not only is each section made up of different professions and skills, but the people within them are responsible to different leaders, each of whom has accepted standards of performance, and of professional conduct, which are perpetuated through training and example.

Into this extremely complex organisation is built a hierarchy. The position which people hold is distinguished, either by forms of address, or, as in the case of nurses, by uniform.

The hospital environment is often characterised by tension. Further pressure is imposed when there are shortages of staff, or when there are many emergency calls which make additional demands. The response with which people react to this situation will depend on their morale and their attitude towards their work, and the *esprit de corps*, both within the groups themselves, and within the hospital as a whole.

Because there is a common objective—"the good of the patient" —and common values—"the highest standard of care for the patient"—this response is usually satisfactory. However, in order that work may continue harmoniously, there must be other factors. The first of these has already been considered, namely the importance of two-way communications, the second is the importance of co-ordination of the various contributions and activities of the groups within the hospital.

It is right that nurses should look beyond their own sphere of activity and see how their contribution affects the organisation as a whole. With a common purpose, there should be unity of action based on mutual respect and understanding of one another's problems. It is easy to concentrate on the differences instead of searching for this common ground and of accepting from colleagues those things which help everyone to make a better contribution.

In some hospitals there are regular meetings of representatives of all the different groups, or informal gatherings of Heads of Departments with the lay and nurse administrators. This is not enough, for it is in the daily contact with one another that good relations grow—or disappear. It requires effort to learn about other people's work and problems, but this is necessary, and a particular responsibility for those in a position of leadership.

It is not possible to look at all the different groups of people who work with nurses in hospital, and because some are omitted it does not mean that they are any less important. However, the few that have been chosen are of special significance.

1. *Medical Staff.* An observer in any hospital ward, quickly notices the relationship between the Doctor and the Sister—especially the Consultant. Sometimes the mutual consideration and appreciation is so outstanding that it provides a very real contribution to the atmosphere generally. On the other hand, there are situations where there is little communication between the two, other than passive obedience from the nurse.

It is interesting to consider what the effect on hospital life would be if all doctors and nurses adopted an attitude of mutual respect which recognised the fact that they are colleagues in the true sense of the word. Would it be possible in these circumstances to see the disappearance of extra beds, and the sharing of available beds throughout the hospital by all consultants?[1] Would there be more consideration of the difficulties of the Theatre Superintendents who are concerned about the state of the theatres because continuous sessions do not allow sufficient time to clean them properly? Would less experienced nurses have the privilege and the enjoyment of hearing all about the patients they are nursing, instead of Sister or her Deputy whose presence is usually demanded by doctors?

Perhaps some of the answers are in the profession's own hands. Have nurses been sufficiently vocal about these things? The maxim that the "nurse never argues, and always obeys" is firmly established in some situations, and fear still exists as a deterrent to better relationships.

As medical knowledge advances, it is inevitable that the demands on the nurse become greater. The nursing profession is making a brave attempt to meet these demands so that the medical staff can use this knowledge to the full. The time has come, however, when it is essential that some of the implications of these advances are faced *together*. Some hospitals have found the establishment of a Medico-Nursing Liaison Committee[2] of great value. This provides a means of discussing informally new treatments and procedures, the ethical aspects and the impact of these on nurse training.

Nurses in charge of Wards and Departments can do much to promote this sharing of responsibility, by bringing the problems to the notice of medical colleagues at an early stage. The medical and nursing views will not always be the same, but nothing but good can come from discussion, and the mutual understanding of one another's difficulties.

2. *Administrative Staff.* The concept of "Tripartite Administration" which formed the substance of the Bradbeer Report[3] has been much criticised, but there is no doubt that where there is co-operation between the nursing and the lay administration, the whole hospital reaps the benefit. Perhaps as some preparatory courses for management become multi-disciplinary, there will be more opportunity to lay the foundations for good relationships. Nurse Administrators must be aware of the matters which they need to share, and be prepared to make time for discussion. It is easy, in the rush of the daily routine, to allow meetings with, for example, the hospital secretary to take second place. However, both nurse and lay administrator must feel that keeping in touch regularly is a necessity. Nurses will often be grateful for the support which comes from a relationship of this kind, particularly when complaints arise from patients or relatives, or there is any question of litigation. If a nursing matter of importance is being brought to Committee, it can be a tremendous help if the hospital secretary has already been given the facts, and understands the implications.

There are many duties which Senior Nurses have now handed to the Hospital Administrator. These include responsibility for Catering, Supplies, and in most instances, the Domestic Management. It is agreed that this is right, as it leaves the professional nurse free to give her time to the needs of the nursing service. However, where the relationship between nursing and other departments is good, consultation on these matters will be frequent, and the nurse's contribution will be welcomed. The welfare of patients embraces so many departments that it is inevitable that there will be overlaps of responsibility. It is when this fact is forgotten that trouble comes. It is not unknown for Ward Sisters to be reluctant to take any further responsibility for ward cleanliness once a Domestic Superintendent has been appointed to the staff of the hospital; and yet it is the nurse, with her expert knowledge of hygiene and the dangers of cross-infection, who can guide those who have not the benefit of this specialised training.

3. *Nurse Planners and Architects.* It may seem strange to some that this group has been included, but it is now unusual if nurses are not in some way involved with the planning of a new hospital or the upgrading of an old one. The Hospital Building Programme has made an impact on the profession, and nurses who are managing the various departments must be ready to tell the architects what

is required if the surroundings are to be such that both they and the patients will benefit.

This means learning to read plans intelligently—terms such as "operational policy" and "outline of function" must be understood. It is at the early stage that the nurse has the greatest contribution to make by telling the hospital planners what is going to be done within each department. This "operational policy" is the keystone around which the structure is built. For example, the Sister in the Outpatient Department who can describe the various requirements for the treatment of patients will enable the architect to know the relationship of the rooms to be built within that area.

Once the new hospitals are built, nurses will be taking part in the commissioning. It is important that sufficient time is allowed for the orientation of staff, so that they can learn how to work in the new building, the method of supplying the wards and departments, communication routes, and the use of staff. Old patterns will not always be possible in different surroundings, and it may be a good opportunity to adopt something different. It must not be forgotten that a strange environment can make people feel very insecure unless they have been shown how to come to terms with it.

Once the building has been in use for a time, it will then be important to assess the design and the equipment in the light of experience, and the service which it has been possible to give to the patients.

4. *The Research Worker.* Only a few nurses are as yet equipped to carry out true research, but it is vital to the growth of the profession that all nurses are "research minded". This means that those in charge must understand what it is all about—not a quick way of finding the answer to problems that baffle us, but a way of assembling information in order that there may be better judgement, and therefore better performance. Nurses do not always find it easy to look at situations objectively, and they fear that a discovery will be made which will undermine confidence or highlight something which is wrong. This difficulty must be overcome in order that benefit may be obtained from the activity of the research worker.

There are now short courses available for nurses to help them to understand research procedures. These can be most valuable, but every nurse in a position of leadership must make the effort to find out the part which she can usefully play if asked to assist in an undertaking of this kind. Suggestions are also needed from these nurses for suitable research projects. It is the person who is doing the job who is often the only one who knows what is required.

5. *The Hospital Chaplain.* In many hospitals the tradition that the Hospital Chaplain is concerned only with the sick, or those who particularly seek help, still prevails. The concept of a minister to the *community* within the hospital has been only half-heartedly accepted. Sometimes the excuse is made that he only represents one denomination but, unfortunately, only too often it is because he is part-time, and has insufficient opportunity. On the other hand, the amount that the Chaplain can give depends on the attitude of those within the hospital to his services. He may act as counsellor to many grades of staff if his supportive role is recognised, and if he is welcomed as part of the hospital team, rather than "someone who occasionally visits from the Church". Informal discussion on subjects which concern all the staff, and lunch-hour talks shared by nurses, medical students, physiotherapists and all who want to come, can be of great value.

6. *The Ancillary Staff.* Sometimes nurses understandably feel that their part is the outstanding one as far as the daily care of the patient goes. In some ways they are right, but they could not do their work without a large group of people who supply them with the tools to do their job, and who provide a service which enables them to be free to exercise their skills. Ward and Departmental Sisters in particular have a responsibility to see that nurses recognise the importance of the contribution made by ancillary staff, so that they are treated with the courtesy and respect which is their due. Many nurses can remember with gratitude a Theatre Porter who whispered what to do next when they first visited the operating theatre, or how grateful they were when Mr. X. was at the switchboard on a particularly busy night; yet these people are not always told how much their services are appreciated.

7. *Voluntary Workers.* More and more work is being done by voluntary helpers, and in some hospitals their work is highly organised. Nurses-in-Charge of the departments where they give their services must make sure that they are welcomed, and that full use is made of their time and skill. Some of them have received quite extensive training, especially those who are members of the National Hospitals Service Reserve, and it is sad when they are not recognised as responsible people, capable of making a useful contribution in the ward team. It is important that the work of untrained helpers is carefully considered, so that they feel that their assistance is worthwhile, but that the patients only receive personal care from those qualified to give it.

REFERENCES

[1] Oxford Regional Hospital Board—Operational Research Unit. *Nursing Times*, 2.9.66, p. 1168.

[2] *Duties and Position of the Nurse*, Royal College of Nursing, and National Council of Nurses of the U.K.

[3] Central Health Services Council—Report of the Committee on the Internal Administration of Hospitals (Bradbeer). H.M.S.O., 1954.

SUGGESTIONS FOR FURTHER READING

"Research and Hospital Management," Anne Crichton, M.A. *The Hospital*, February 1966, p. 66.

Commissioning New Hospital Buildings. Report of the King Edward Hospital Fund, 1966.

CHAPTER 8

COMMUNICATIONS AND GOOD RELATIONS
(*Continued*)

"WHAT I should advocate and like to see encouraged is a generation of nurses who have been not only *trained* during their hospital years, but developed as personalities. They would be developed as thinkers and as speakers, so that they could communicate sufficiently to shape the world around them."[1] These words were written recently in the Nursing Press, and challenged the ability of members of the nursing profession to contribute to the life of the community. It was suggested that hitherto nurses have confined themselves to an existence inside the hospital, allowing little time or energy for expressing themselves in any way outside. The situation is, of course, changing. Now many nurses are non-resident and entering much more fully into "ordinary" life. It is encouraging to hear of nurses undertaking civic responsibilities and widening their interests.

Difficulties have sometimes arisen because off-duty is uncertain; and in the past nurses may have been anxious that "outside" activities, if undertaken too seriously, would be detrimental to their work, since the time available was so scanty. However, the shorter working week has altered this picture, and nurses responsible for arranging the duty rotas have an obligation to ensure that off-duty periods are known in good time so that they can be used to advantage.

With the changes that are taking place in the pattern of patient care, there will be increasing demands on the goodwill of the public. Five-Day Wards, Day Hospitals, and Day Beds, all ask more of the relatives, even if support is forthcoming from the local authority services. Now that so much more can be done for the elderly sick, more families will be asked to care for ageing relatives who have been restored to some kind of reasonable activity. The response will be so much better if those in the community understand the aims and activities of the hospital through knowing those who work there.

There are some specific ways in which the nurse who is in a position of responsibility within the hospital can spread her influence beyond it, and assist in building up these good relations.

1. INFORMATION TO THE PUBLIC

In most instances, factual information to the public will be provided by the hospital administrator, assisted in some instances by a Public Relations Officer. However, there are occasions when the

Senior Nurse Administrators may be asked by the Press to describe some nursing activity or recent change in policy. Sometimes they have been reluctant to undertake this, because they fear that either the information will be incorrectly reported, or that there may be undue publicity. If, however, the confidence and appreciation of the Press can be won, they will almost certainly give a fair deal in return. As a safeguard, it is wise to provide a summary, in writing, of what is said. This can be particularly useful if a speech is to be reported.

The importance of accuracy cannot be over-emphasised. Both discretion and diplomacy are needed and, this is a responsibility which cannot be ignored or taken lightly.

These remarks equally apply to occasions when nurses are asked to partake in a broadcast or television programme. If filming is to take place in a hospital ward, the nurse responsible must be sure that too much strain is not put on either staff or patients, since this can be a very exhausting process.

2. LISTENING TO COMPLAINTS

Even with the greatest care, there will be occasions when complaints from patients or their relatives are received. However trivial or unjustified they may seem, it is essential that they are taken seriously, and investigated promptly and efficiently. Sometimes the complaint may come in writing from an overwrought relative who has recently been bereaved. In this case, it is far better to ask the person concerned to come and discuss the problem, than to persist with the inquiry by correspondence. Troubles can often be cleared up quite speedily in this way, and help can be given at the same time. The Nurse Administrator or Ward Sister who is faced with this kind of problem is wise to spend time in listening to the grievance, and not to try to justify the action of the hospital staff at the outset. When all the facts are collected the matter can be dealt with logically, and with the sympathy it deserves, in collaboration with the Hospital Administrator.

3. PUBLIC SPEAKING

An invitation to present the prizes at the local school, to open the church bazaar or to talk about some aspect of the job—there are many calls on the experienced nurse, and some may think it worthwhile to have some special training in the art of speaking in public. However, there is much that nurses can do to help themselves.

The natural fear of appearing on a platform can be largely overcome if the speaker can forget herself and her own feelings, and concentrate on the talk which is to be given, and those who are to benefit. There is no doubt that public speaking becomes easier with practice, and that confidence grows with experience. However, it is always wise to spend time on the preparation of the speech or talk, and to find out exactly what is required: the length of the talk, and if there is to be time set aside for questions and discussion. It is also necessary to know the type of audience, since the same presentation will not be suitable for all groups.

The introduction must be sufficiently interesting to make an appeal to the audience, and also to give them some idea of the objective. A few well placed words at this point can make all the difference to the success of the talk.

Having written the headings, the material and substance can be inserted. If there are to be any quotations it is wise to write these in full with the references. Some people like to make very full notes, others can manage with a brief outline and sub-headings—much depends on the skill and experience of the speaker. Postcards are very suitable for these notes since they can be held in the hand at the correct distance without holding the head down. If the notes are more extensive, it is a good plan to ask for a lectern.

Many speakers fail to satisfy their audience because they do not manage to throw their voice to the back of the room; it is useful to concentrate on some particular object, and then to direct the voice towards it. It is also worthwhile beginning by asking the audience if they can hear should there be any doubt. If a microphone is to be used, is is wise to practice beforehand, and learn the tricks which it can play with the voice. It can be very disconcerting if the speaker is unfamiliar with its use.

The audience should be left in no doubt of the purpose of the talk, and the closing sentences should be a summary of the points which are to be remembered.

Votes of Thanks. Giving a vote of thanks is a privilege, and a public duty which should not be shirked. If an approach is made at the beginning of a meeting, this will provide an opportunity to make a few notes during the proceedings. If, however, there is advanced notice, the invitation should be accepted gladly, and the opportunity taken to find out any interesting points, to which reference can be made, about the person in question.

There are many ways in which nurses can partake in the life of the community and, as citizens, they can think them out for themselves. Sometimes they will act as an official representative of the hospital, sometimes as an individual. Whatever the occasion, the nurse's responsibility as a professional person cannot be ignored. Perhaps it can best be summed up in the remark of the taxi driver who, passing the local hospital, jerked his head towards the front door and said to his passenger—"That's our Matron—she's lovely!"

REFERENCE

[1] "Baffled Energy—The Nurse and the Community," P. M. Jones. *Nursing Times*, 19.8.66, p. 1107.

SUGGESTION FOR FURTHER READING

"Meeting and Speaking," Marjorie Hellier, I.G.S.M. *Nursing Times*, Reprint, June-August 1955.

PART THREE

MEETING THE NEEDS
OF THE
INDIVIDUAL

Professions like nations can only flourish through an individual sense of corporate responsibility.

Florence Nightingale

CHAPTER 9

JOB SATISFACTION

THE nurse who leads and manages other people cannot do so effectively unless she has a very real sense of the personal worth of each individual. This means rejecting autocratic leadership which dominates a situation and expects passive obedience; instead, the leader adopts a supportive role which encourages each member of the group to be self-reliant and to participate actively in the work on hand.

This supportive role must not be confused with weakness or lack of determination; on the contrary, it makes it possible for everyone to work towards their goal, and to find personal satisfaction in doing so.

What is it that people look for in order to find happiness and contentment in their work? Five essentials have been chosen for discussion—readers will probably think of others, but these are among the most important.

1. A sense of security.
2. Opportunity for initiative and progress.
3. Support and encouragement.
4. A sense of achievement.
5. Discipline and justice.

1. *A Sense of Security.* Why do certain areas of a hospital gain a reputation as happy or unhappy places to work in? It must be acknowledged that a certain amount of pleasure—or apprehension —is experienced by a newcomer according to the commonly held view about the various departments. The ward which is known to be a "good" one has the advantage that nurses come with a feeling that all will be well, and they feel secure from the beginning. On the other hand, those who are anticipating trouble will be on the watch for it, and may find it difficult to settle.

It has already been noted that the tone of the department is set by the leader, and Professor Revans has shown that the attitudes of the nursing team are a reflection of those held by the Ward Sister.[1] Atmosphere is made up of all kinds of intangibles, and everyone contributes. It is strange how people with different backgrounds and varying qualities and gifts, can together create the "right climate". Much will depend, however, on the Nurse-in-Charge.

Knowing that she can only influence her group for eight hours of the day, she will realise that other influences will also be at work, and will learn to accept them as they are. She will study each member and, assuming that there is much that is good in everybody, will search for those qualities and allow them to develop.

Where there is security, the group can rely on their leader being absolutely fair. They will know, that even if things go wrong, she has the maturity and poise to deal with the situation without allowing her opinions or her mood to influence her attitude towards other people. Much harm can be made by "chain reactions" which occur when the person at the top has been unable to control resentment or dissatisfaction, and has passed this down the line. When times of stress due to external pressures and tensions do come, the good leader will provide the serenity and guidance which will help the group through this period, and give them the necessary stimulus to face their difficulties.

This kind of atmosphere can thrive even where there is an established hierarchy. There is no need to have familiarity in order to break down any barriers which may exist: a professional climate is not incompatible with good relations so long as there is an understanding of the need to love and to be loved. The latter must not be misunderstood. Everyone needs to feel wanted, and to enjoy a sense of belonging, but this is not the same as wanting to be liked. Sometimes the desire to please others has been directed towards personal popularity, but the truly great leaders have found that it is not possible to be all things to all men. However, the leader who is respected will gain co-operation even when asking for participation in an unpopular, or unpleasant task. People like Edward Wilson, and Dr. Ida Scudder gathered round them small groups willing to overcome enormous difficulties in order to achieve their goals. They were in no way weak personalities, and they were greatly loved.

Security is experienced, therefore, when the members of the group and their leader enjoy a mutual trust. It must not be forgotten, however, that security embraces things also. It is essential that each individual can be reasonably confident about future prospects, and have freedom from financial anxiety. Appointments to the staff should be confirmed in writing, and should convey the responsibility which the post entails. These matters are all-important if there is to be peace of mind.

2. *Opportunity for Initiative and Progress.* "I wish people would understand that, although we may have had little experience, we are not unintelligent!" This comment was made by a young student

nurse wanting most desperately to have the opportunity to prove herself. In nursing, the delegation of responsibility often falls into two extremes, either too much is given too soon, without adequate supervision and help, or nurses ready for a challenge are starved of opportunity.

Anyone who has had the opportunity to interview or talk with an eighteen-year-old, just about to begin her training, cannot help but be struck by two things: firstly a keen desire to help others, and secondly, enthusiasm. Sadly, it sometimes happens that this initial zeal is dampened, and nurses become discouraged because they are not treated as responsible people. If they are to find satisfaction in their work and also take a full part in their profession when qualified, they must learn how to observe, discriminate and, in the light of experience, make decisions.

Perhaps difficulties arise because of a failure to recognise ability. A post-certificate nurse may come for further training and, because the Sister or Staff Nurse has not taken the trouble to find out the ground that she has already covered, precious time and tempers may be lost by "talking down" to the nurse, and failing to give her scope. There is also a danger that others may be held back because the Nurse-in-Charge lacks confidence in herself, and discourages questions because she fears she may not know the answers. It is impossible to know everything, but the fundamentals on which the work is founded must be mastered. Occasionally, there may be failure to delegate because the senior nurse quite unjustifiably fears for her own position. She may consider that the person who is particularly outstanding will prove to be a rival if given the opportunity to take responsibility. This is a tragic situation, and can cause untold trouble and unhappiness.

It may happen that the Ward Sister or Staff Nurse is only too ready to delegate, but she finds less experienced nurses afraid to come forward. There is the "silent" person who fears she will not measure up to what is expected of her; and the "lone wolf" who prefers to carry on quietly on her own, but who misses the joy which teamwork can bring. This situation can be found at more senior levels also. In such instances, the stimulus must come either from the leader herself or from a carefully chosen colleague who is prepared to help. Much can be gained by bringing everyone in the team together for informal discussion. This provides an opportunity for airing problems, and for putting over the purpose involved. It must be *"our"* venture, seen as work which is done together, with one end in view. The leader of this group will need to be prepared to accept criticism, and to listen to grievances, but will have the opportunity to turn these towards a positive objective. Everyone needs to let off steam at some time, but this must never be allowed to become negative or destructive. However what may be required most will probably be a sense of humour as, when a group has had the opportunity to laugh together, there is more chance that they will see their work as something which is to be enjoyed.

In the past there has been a tendency to require a nurse to be always "on the go", but this takes away from her a most precious freedom. She must have time to talk to patients, and to do a good job if her work is to be truly satisfying. Time and opportunity go hand in hand. When someone begins to search—either for knowledge or the chance to be more useful—there is, in front of her, the joy of discovery. This is when the job holds the challenge which is the life-blood of success and satisfaction.

3. *Support and Encouragement.* "I have tried to help her, but she does not seem to want it!" There are those who will put on a brave face because they feel they ought to do so, and they do not want to let the side down—they usually get into more trouble, and make further mistakes. There are some who are difficult to help because they put up a barrier and will not let others in—these are the people who probably need help the most. It may never be known why the barrier went up. It may be something personal which others have no business to know but sometimes, if the way is left open, it can be shared. This person cannot be ignored, although it may demand much time and effort if she is to be helped. However, any trouble taken will be well rewarded.

In life, there are those who can quite well fend for themselves and there are those who need extra help and encouragement. It is necessary, therefore, to understand the "make-up" of the individual to know where this support is needed. Treating everyone alike does not work, because human beings are not alike. On the other hand, this is not to be confused with favouritism which cannot be condoned.

An opportunity to recognise work which has been well done should never be missed. If the praise can be given in front of others on the spot it may have added value, so long as the moment is chosen carefully. Particular encouragement and praise may be needed by those who have less spectacular tasks, and feel that their contribution is somewhat inferior to that of others. Such a situation may sometimes be found in the long-stay geriatric wards where devoted nursing care, which may seem to have little reward, is given.

Now that so many special units for treatment are established, it is as well for senior nurses to realise how depressing some of this work can be, and the demands which it can make emotionally. The strain of constant and meticulous observation can be very great, and the staff of these wards may need considerable encouragement and understanding.

Sometimes things will go wrong, and these are the occasions when support is required the most. Whatever happens the nurse must be upheld in front of the patient, and the matter dealt with in privacy as soon as possible afterwards. It has not been unknown for a nurse to lose all confidence, and even to give up her career, because the necessary support was not given after she had made a mistake. The administration of a wrong drug is a very serious matter, and nobody would deny this, but there are ways of handling these situations which can help the offender to realise the implications without destroying either self-confidence or self-respect. All the facts must be collected before deciding who is to blame. If a young student or pupil nurse fails to carry out a treatment which is beyond that which should be expected of her in the light of her experience, it will be the person who delegated this responsibility who will be to blame. The vital question which must be asked is "*Why* did this happen?" More experienced staff need support too, and if they have this they will be more prepared to meet their problems and deal with them.

4. *Sense of Achievement.* Perhaps there is nothing more satisfying than the knowledge that you have been able to help someone. Yet, so often, nurses are deprived of this satisfaction by keeping them busy on a ceaseless round of activity—known as "job assignment." This allows little opportunity for taking part in the patient's recovery except in a piecemeal fashion. There are many excuses made for this: shortage of staff, the geography of the ward, and so on. Many of these points are valid, but "my patient" can mean so much more to the nurse—and to the patient also—and can help her to consider him as a person, and to think out for herself his individual needs. Organisation of the ward activities through "group assignment" can increase the sense of responsibility among the ward team, and also provide better continuity of care for the patient.

With the grouping of hospitals and the building of the large District Hospital, it will be important to consider the "areas of control". Division of the work will be essential to good management, and some far-seeing nurse administrators have already allocated clinical areas of responsibility to their assistants. This not only provides more satisfaction to the experienced and often highly-qualified nurse, but keeps her in touch with the patients and staff, thus increasing her usefulness.

5. *Discipline and Justice.* There may be some who will be surprised to find these included. The two are not only inseparable,

but they are absolutely necessary for the "right" climate which has been mentioned previously. The majority of people, with good reason, prefer some discipline, providing that it is administered fairly.

The nursing profession has been much criticised for its "outworn discipline", and it is therefore important to consider carefully what is necessary, acceptable, and right, not only for executing professional responsibilities, but also to help nurses to become responsible citizens. The ultimate aim should be the exercise of a personal discipline not enforced as something which has to be tolerated, but welcomed as a necessary aid to living.

Wherever there is a large group of people living and working together, there must be discipline. The rules need to be few, justifiable, and it must be possible to keep them. It is no good insisting there is less noise, unless equipment is provided which allows this, and which is serviced regularly. The requests which are made should be recognised as obligations which concern the good of everyone, and those who make them must be prepared to see that they are obeyed. There are times, however, when a relaxation of what is laid down can be acceptable. The wise leader knows when this is possible without relinquishing principles, and that there is less likelihood that people will take advantage if they know that rules will not be used unfairly. They will be even more co-operative if they are trusted.

The importance of self-discipline has already been mentioned, and this is essential if standards are to be maintained. Nurses in control need to be firm where there is inefficiency, for it is so easy for one step backwards to lead down the hill. It is necessary to ask why this person is not keeping her standard, and to take the trouble to search for the problems and put them right. It must be accepted, however, that there will be faults, and the perfectionist may only produce frustration. There is also a danger sometimes that, in her anxiety to maintain a good reputation, the Nurse-in-Charge may anticipate trouble when there is none intended. Preconceived ideas about people and their ability can lead to much unhappiness, opinions can only be based on a just assessment of the facts, and not on hearsay. There will always be the "problem child", but this is the opportunity to give extra guidance and help.

It is well known that, where a high standard is required, the response is usually greater, and nurses, if they are asked to participate, are no exception. Most nurses genuinely want to take a pride in their performance, and are willing to accept that correction is a necessary part of learning, and contributes to better work next time. Their response will depend on the way the correction is given.

However, while there is no doubt that discipline should be maintained in a congenial atmosphere there will be occasions when the nurse in a position of leadership will have to deal with grievances. Problems of this nature need to be settled promptly, although never before all the facts are known. It is a wise plan to get the two sides together, and help them to talk out their differences—and it is surprising how often this will be all that is required. Sometimes it will be more serious, and it may be necessary to obtain information from a witness, or the person who is in control of the particular department. Quite often, troubles have arisen because of the particular stress of the moment, and the senior nurse should be quick to recognise undue strain which may need to be relieved by additional help, or even a period of rest. The situation may not only be aggravated by circumstances, but also by incompatible personalities, and help may be required from a higher authority. It is well to make a note of what is said during the interview, and if the grievances are persistently occurring in one department, this may be an indication that further action is required.

In attempting to put right that which has gone wrong, the Nurse-in-Charge may occasionally be faced with the need to impose some form of deterrent, although this will be rare. She must be careful to make sure that it is not herself, and her pride which is hurt, and to be certain that whatever course of action is taken is absolutely just.

There are several factors which should influence the decision about how to deal with the offender. Firstly, did she know she was doing wrong? Was it intentional? Is she a persistent offender, or is this the first time? Are other people involved, and what is the extent of the damage? Did she own up, and apologise? Is the apology genuine, and is she really penitent? If any form of punishment is considered it must be educative, or it is valueless. It is better if the offender's attitude and behaviour can be influenced and changed for the good. There are many ways of doing this: by working with the person or by appointing someone else to do so; by talking and persuading them; or perhaps best of all, by giving them a challenge so that they can feel that those in authority still have faith in them and trust them. It may be that such an action by the leader is just what is needed.

In trying to analyse the factors that contribute to job satisfaction, much stress has been laid on the contribution made by those in control, and this may appear a large demand. However, the nurse who is prepared to give all her effort towards the well-being of her team will find that loyalty and status do not come through holding her particular position, but that they are both earned, and are part of her own reward and satisfaction.

REFERENCE

[1] *Standards for Morale—Cause and Effect in Hospitals,* R. W. Revans, 1964. Published for the Nuffield Provincial Hospitals Trust by Oxford University Press.

SUGGESTIONS FOR FURTHER READING

Nursing Team Leadership by T. Kron, R.N.I. Published by W. B. Saunders Co., London and Philadelphia, 1961.

"The Development of Identity with the Role of the Nurse," Dr. J. Macguire. *International Journal of Nursing Studies,* Vol. 3, No. 3, p. 137. September 1966.

Education—Some Fundamental Problems, A. G. Hughes and E. H. Hughes. Published by Longmans. Chapter 8, "Discipline".

SUGGESTIONS FOR FURTHER STUDY

1. Does insecurity exist among the various grades of nursing staff in hospital, if so, why? What can be done to help by exercising good management?

2. "A disciplined person is someone who has become a willing disciple or learner in the various activities of life." How can this statement become a reality for nurses in training?

CHAPTER 10

THE PATTERN OF GUIDANCE

WHO is the best person to give guidance? This is a question which is being asked quite frequently in hospital today. In America, counsellors are often employed for this purpose, but in this country the tendency has been to consider that this kind of a specialist is not required, so long as heads of departments are alert to the needs of their team, and are approachable and accessible.

The pattern may alter, and this provision may be supplemented by, for example, an Occupational Health Service for all members of the staff. There will, however, always be the need for senior nurses to give help and guidance to those for whom they are responsible when it is required. They must have their general welfare at heart, for this is an essential part of good management.

Nurse Administrators and Tutors have to convince Committees that good accommodation, adequate "changing facilities" and sufficient sanitary annexes are of vital importance. This is sometimes very difficult when there are so many calls on a limited financial budget, but Committee members have to be educated to think beyond the routine medical care of the staff to those things which contribute to *positive* health. The nurses themselves must be aware of the hazards they may meet, so that they can teach others the precautions to be taken; and equipment must be provided which will prevent trauma and accidents. More hoists are needed, for example, for lifting incapacitated patients, and adjustable height beds.

However, these are not the only kind of problems which concern the nursing staff of a busy hospital; the senior members of staff, who carry heavy responsibilities, are themselves often in need of help. Their task can be a lonely one, and sharing the burden can bring great relief. It may be that the difficulties are of a domestic nature or concern personal matters, and advice given in an unpatronising way can make all the difference.

The art of giving guidance is firstly to be a good listener, then to be able to assess the problem, and and lastly to lead the person who is in trouble to come to her own decision. She will have sought help because she feels she can trust and respect her adviser. This is why people must be free to choose to whom they wish to go. This mutual confidence is essential if there is to be a positive result.

On occasions, the more experienced nurse will be asked for advice by the younger members of the profession, or she may realise that they need help and do not wish to seek it for various reasons. What are the senior nurses responsibilities towards those who are still in training? Do we know what they want?

This is a difficult subject, but it may be worthwhile giving it consideration, in an attempt to find out some of the ways in which the nurse in a position of leadership can help the younger members of her team.

SOME OF THE PROBLEMS

It cannot be easy to grow up in modern society. There are pressures on all sides—material affluence, criticism of established ideals, and the influence of television and the cinema. These have opened up new ideas which may be troublesome, and yet hard to resist. Although they can count on freedom from many of the ills which used to beset the community, young people have now to contend with the insecurity which results from the existence of nuclear weapons and the horrors of modern warfare.

The hopes and fears of youth are unique to their age—and this is an age of uncertainty. What is needed therefore, is stability—something to which they can turn, which will be dependable and safe. There are many ways, which have already been discussed, in which the environment can be made more secure, but nurses in training could be greatly helped if more effort were to be made to marry their educational needs with the demands of the nursing service. With thought and perseverance this can be arranged, and reports have shown that the uncertainty of ward allocation can affect the student adversely, leading to wastage during training.[1, 2]

The seemingly confident young adult of today has other fears. Many of them spring from an awareness of the greater opportunities that life holds, and they are afraid they will not be allowed to reach out and grasp them. They are conscious of physical and mental growth, and of a new-found freedom. They instinctively rebel against anything which might curb this. Frequent requests from nurses to be non-resident and the resentment of any suggestion of regimentation in the Nurse's Hostel are an illustration of this point. This change from dependence to independence must be accepted, but at the same time young people may need help to realise that discipline and freedom go together, because there will always be limitations imposed by the world in which they live, and obligations to the rest of the community.

THE SIGNS OF MATURITY

This journey towards independence means that there is more and more freedom of choice, and the adolescent is increasingly free to conduct her life in the way she wishes. However, none of us lives in isolation, and every privilege carries with it a responsibility towards other people, which is accepted by the mature person. This includes developing tolerance, overcoming prejudice, and gaining control of personal emotions. It means coming to terms with oneself which will instil confidence, a sense of values, and will give rise to a way of life. Social skills have to be learnt in order to meet the challenge of personal relationships, and there must be a conscious effort to take one's place in the community with poise and serenity. The mature person is ready to accept the ideas of other people, and yet to be free of their influence if they are contrary to what is considered right and wise. People mature at varying times of life, and their environment and background have considerable influence.

The following however, is a list of some factors which could be used as a tentative guide in considering whether a young person has reached this goal.

1. Is she equipped to obtain and hold a job?
2. Is she equipped to take her place in any social group in which she may find herself?
3. Has she thought through to a sensible and constructive attitude about other people and the opposite sex?
4. Has she found some kind of faith, belief or values?
5. Has she accepted responsibility for her own actions, and the effect they may have on other people?

In helping young people to grow to maturity, leaders have to search out the vital factors which affect standards and values and not to confuse them with petty detail or personal likes or dislikes. This is where the maturity of the leader herself, and her own ability to be tolerant and understanding takes first place.

OPPORTUNITIES FOR GUIDANCE

An appeal for help may come in many disguises. It may be by abnormal behaviour—such as precocious claims for attention, an immature response to difficulties which have arisen, or a general falling off of standards. It is for the nurse who is in charge and controlling her group to be on the alert to recognise what is happening, and then to offer help as unobtrusively as possible. Sometimes it will be refused, and then she can only wait and watch for another opportunity. It is important to be accessible during such times, and to be sure to display no visible shock when an approach is made.

When the person comes, it may be that firm loyalties will prevent her from saying very much, and it is on these occasions that reassurance is required on the question of keeping confidences. On the other hand, if the trouble affects the group as a whole, it may be necessary to point out the unhappiness which may persist through misplaced loyalties.

All efforts to guide or comfort will be useless unless nurse leaders have themselves worked out their own philosophy for life, and know what they believe to be right, and why. It may be that the person who has come for help is subconsciously asking for guidance. The aim should be to let her see that she need not be alone and that in the sharing of the problem, the signposts may become visible— although she must discover the actual pathway for herself.

Finally, it is important to remember that young people can become physically and mentally exhausted whilst trying to sort themselves out, and it may be that time and rest are all that is required.

OPPORTUNITIES FOR LEISURE

Leisure occupations should be of the individual's own choosing, and guidance will only be required to the extent that opportunities are given to take part in activities which are rewarding. There are some members of the profession who do not consider that the provision of recreational facilities is part of the Nurse Administrator's responsibility. They argue that, with so many nurses non-resident, few take advantage of them. This may be true, but on the other hand there will always be some—particularly in the younger age groups—who need stimulus and encouragement. Where there is insufficient outlet for initiative and creative energy, it can be channelled in the wrong direction. The Nurse-in-Charge can motivate, and provide the opportunity—the choice can still be an individual one. Some hospitals have appointed Social Secretaries to give this help. These people are well equipped for their task, and can supply all the information to suit every taste. Sometimes it is to the Social Secretary that the nurse will turn to talk about her own thoughts and feelings, and she may get to know her very well. For instance, dances and parties with medical students will get off to a good start with the assistance of such a person who, whilst giving the nurses the freedom to organise in their own way, can provide the necessary guidance.

One of the reasons why it is important that nurses know how to use their leisure, is that it should provide an opportunity for the development of their own personalities. Whatever form it takes, it should give mental satisfaction and refreshment. It is necessary to bring something of the individual's own creative spirit, or some part of the personality and imagination, into the activity which is being enjoyed.

Recreation and leisure also bring people into the company of others, and from a narrow circle into a much wider one. It can provide an opportunity for team spirit, and allows the more mature and forward person to use her energy in taking responsibility for her colleagues. It is important that this is recognised, so that the potential leaders are not frustrated; and, finding no satisfaction for their enthusiasm and gifts, are tempted to use them wrongly.

Some people find it hard to mix, and there can be very real home-sickness among young folk who have left home for the first time. Off-duty for them can be a real problem. Either through lack of knowledge about what there is to do, or fear of a strange large city, nurses often waste their time by staying in their own rooms—they may even join in undesirable activities for want of something better to do. Senior nurses both in hospital and the School of Nursing have a duty to help these newcomers to find friends, perhaps by introducing them to colleagues who have come from the same town or country, and by encouraging them to give them a helping hand during the early months.

The nurse from overseas deserves special mention. Very many girls—and some boys—have been welcomed as students from other countries, but in many instances little is done to help them on arrival to become orientated to a new and strange life. They are expected to conform but they are at a loss to know how to meet what is asked of them. Their anxiety sometimes makes them afraid to explain their difficulties. It is for senior nurses to meet these anxieties at the earliest possible moment, and to try to understand the problems of finding friends, of different food and a strange climate, and of the many other situations which confront them. In addition, language may be a barrier, and guidance must be available for those who have not mastered this sufficiently to embark on training. It can mean much to the overseas student if he or she is introduced to the local church of the right denomination, and the hospital Chaplain can often give considerable help.

Before leaving the subject of finding friends, it should be mentioned that, on occasions, it may be necessary to give advice when a young nurse develops a friendship which becomes exclusive, and therefore tends to isolate her from the rest of society. This nearly always happens without the person concerned being aware of it, and a tactful word can often save them from much unhappiness. It may be helpful to point out that this is a form of selfishness, since it deprives others of their friendship. The leader can show that she understands that some friendships are closer and more intimate than others, and that these may be very wonderful in themselves, but that, at the same time, it is necessary to make new friends who will enrich their lives and bring new interest and companionship.

In conclusion, nurses who hold responsible and senior appointments within the hospital, must also make sure that they use *their* leisure wisely. Recreation should be *re*-creation—an opportunity to find new strength and energy, and to refresh both mind and body, thus enabling them to return to their work better equipped.

REFERENCES

[1] "Wastage, Sickness and Allocation," E. R. Bendall, *Nursing Times*, 1.6.65, page 760.

[2] *From Student to Nurse.* A study of Student Nurses in Training at Five Schools of Nursing. Oxford A.N.T.C., 1966.

SUGGESTIONS FOR FURTHER READING

"The New Student," R. F. Merivale, R.N.T. *Nursing Times*, 7.6.63, page 704.

"Freedom and Responsibility for Nursing Students," Dorothy Mereness. *American Journal of Nursing*, Vol. 67, No. 1, January 1967.

CHAPTER 11

OPPORTUNITIES FOR LEARNING

THIS section would be incomplete without some reference to the responsibility which the nurse should take towards making opportunities both for herself and others, for learning. It is proposed therefore, to discuss briefly the reasons why this is necessary, and to suggest some of the situations which should be recognised as providing the material which is required.

WHY GO ON LEARNING?

Many nurses remember the feeling of ecstasy on becoming State Registered. The goal had been attained, and the examinations were over. This was the opportunity to sit back and close the books!

The feeling did not last, however, for it soon became apparent that State Registration is like passing a driving test, and only qualifies to take the car on the road. It does not necessarily mean that the driver knows how to deal with every tricky situation he may meet on the highway. Education is a continuous process— or should be, enabling people not only to know their job, with all its technical detail, but to increase their capacity to think, to reason, and to come to decisions.

The dangers of "arm-chair" thinking are well known. It is based only on past and present experience, and embraces none of the stimulus produced by the thoughts of others which can be gained only by personal contact, or by reading. This narrowness is the beginning of unenlightened leadership and, if it is allowed to persist, can only bring disaster. It is essential to undertake our own self-improvement to increase our usefulness, since unprepared minds are unable to recognise opportunities when they appear.

Helping others to learn. In this country much emphasis is laid on the value of practical experience on the job, both for those in training, and for those who have qualified. The new syllabus of training of the General Nursing Council makes it quiet clear that theoretical and practical instruction go hand in hand. In Schools of Nursing, those responsible for education and service need to come even closer together in order to provide the student or pupil nurse with satisfying clinical experience which is of educational value. In the wards and departments, nurses have to develop a frame of mind which is constantly alive to opportunities to pass on knowledge and skill, and this can only be done if Sisters and Staff Nurses have a very clear conception of what is required. Getting together with the Tutors who are responsible for the training programme is the only way to ensure that what is taught in the School of Nursing and the wards is complementary. This is essential if trainees are to feel secure and have confidence in their teachers. Of equal importance is the selection of nurses for training, and also of qualified staff. Nurse Administrators and Tutors have a duty to see that they are able to benefit from the knowledge they acquire. Failure to do this not only wastes valuable professional time, but it can expose patients to risks by placing them under the care of people who are unable to carry out instructions, and understand their needs.

LEARNING SITUATIONS

These should be considered in relation to all grades of staff, but Nurses-in-Charge must know how to discriminate, so that situations are chosen which are suitable, and can therefore be used to advantage.

1. *The Daily Routine.* "Whatever we do, we are always teaching!" This comment has often been made by experienced nurses, and to some extent it is true that, consciously or unconsciously, there are opportunities to teach by example throughout the day's work. What must be understood, however, is that this does not necessarily mean that others are learning. This depends both on the person carrying out the procedure, and the recipient.

"Though people can learn by working—incidentally or intentionally—the right kind of learning or the desired learning takes place only when the learning is planned and systematically directed towards clearly stated objectives, and when clear differentiation is made between what is working routine, and what is method of education."[1]

As a result of staff shortages, and insufficient qualified nurses in the wards, much learning is still done by trial and error. This is always wasteful, since faulty technique has to be corrected, and there can be trauma to both patient and nurse when they have had to grapple with a situation which is beyond them. The remedy partly lies in sorting out the priorities, so that experienced help and supervision are available at the right moment. This means careful organisation of the daily routine, so that there is a recognised plan which withstands the upset of unforeseen emergencies.

2. *A Time of Change.* This provides an excellent opportunity to learn. An outstanding example is the positive approach to Geriatric

Nursing which has opened up a wide field of new knowledge and experience for nurses.

Further opportunities will come as new hospitals are opened, and the staff are shown the principles underlying centralised services and the operational policies for wards and departments. Those responsible for the commissioning have a unique chance to introduce new thinking and progressive ideas.

3. *Contact with People.* Sometimes in an anxiety to explain about the material things, nurses forget how much they can do to promote understanding of other people and their reactions. They have, of course, to be able to understand their own response to different situations if they are to be truly helpful. Much can be learnt about this from colleagues in the psychiatric field who have studied the subject more deeply. "She (the nurse) must like and trust her own spontaneous reaction to situations and people, and be willing to reveal these face to face."[2] The writer of these words was concerned that this vital part of professional training should not be left out—it is of little use if minds are educated and not hearts.

Contact with other people can also help nurses to express themselves. The importance of being articulate has already been mentioned in a previous chapter, but it must not be forgotten that "words themselves can be a barrier to learning". If they are not used properly, or are misinterpreted the learning situation cannot be truly productive.

4. *Opportunity to Observe and Think.* Knowledge is acquired through the use of all the senses. What is seen, contributes to the store of experience and can be used to assess a situation provided it is interpreted in the light of previous knowledge, and is therefore meaningful.

5. *Opportunity to Read.* Some Nursing School Libraries are excellent, but in some places there is room for improvement since both qualified nurses and trainees require the facilities of a good library and access to journals and memoranda. There is a good deal of information which comes into hospitals which never reaches the people who need to know. It is for the Nurse Administrators and Tutors to make sure that Ministry of Health Circulars and other Reports and Surveys, are available to qualified staff. Only in this way can they be alive to the developments which are taking place in the Service and the profession.

Books are expensive, and nurses must therefore make it worthwhile for the authorities to provide them. It is sometimes said that there is no time to read, especially when so many senior nursing staff are married, and occupied with home commitments. However, every professional nurse has an obligation to make an opportunity to read, since this is not a luxury to be indulged in by a few, but a necessity for everyone. In one part of the country, there has been an attempt to meet this difficulty by providing "quick reading" courses for qualified nurses at a local Technical College. There is an art in being able pick out the important and relevant material in order to concentrate on this, and put it to use.

IN-SERVICE TRAINING

Considerable attention is now being given to the question of post-certificate training for nurses, and a recent report has shown the importance of providing this on a sound educational basis, with integration of theoretical and practical instruction.[3] Although there will be active participation at ward and departmental level, these Courses do not come into the same category as In-service training, which is more informal, and should be supplied for certain groups of staff within the hospital. Some of this instruction will be in the form of orientation, or aimed at helping a specific group (e.g. newly-qualified staff nurses), or used as refresher training for those who have been in post for a length of time.

There has been discussion from time to time in an attempt to decide who is responsible for In-service training. Whilst it is most important to enlist the help and guidance of the Nurse Tutors, experienced teachers cannot be expected to spend time and energy on the detailed organisation of, for example, the training of nursing auxiliaries. This kind of course can be satisfactorily undertaken in the ward if it is carefully planned, but it will be of little use if it consists of a few haphazard sessions with no meaning or continuity. The programme should aim at preparing a group of people for a specific task or responsibility. It must be attractive, interesting, and seen to be of use. Unless it has proved to be worthwhile and relevant in content, there will be no enthusiasm among the staff, and it will be considered a waste of time. The following are some points which are worth keeping in mind:

1. Consider carefully what is to be achieved.
2. What do the people concerned feel they require?
3. Decide on the length of the Course, Study Day or Session.
4. Choose the speakers carefully—certain people will appeal to different groups.
5. Leave time for discussion—and plan to allow the group to participate as much as possible.
6. Decide if there are to be visits, practical sessions, whether visual aids are required, etc.

7. Announce the programme as soon as possible, give notice of place, time, off-duty arrangements, whether to attend in mufti, etc.
8. Remember catering arrangements.
9. When the Course is finished, look at it critically, invite comments from those who took part, and make notes for adjustments next time.

This is a very brief summary, and readers with experience will think of other essential details, but the main purpose of identifying these points, is to demonstrate that a considerable effort has to be made if this kind of training is to be of value. Those who have taken part should feel refreshed, stimulated and better informed. They should have increased in confidence, efficiency and, most important, they should have learnt to know their colleagues better.

REFERENCES

[1] *Guide for In-Service Education of Nursing Personnel,* Ingrid Hamelin. W.H.O., Geneva, 1967.

[2] "Lets look at the Teacher," Sidney Jourard, Ph.D. *International Nursing Review,* Oct. 1964, Vol. II, No. 5, p. 45.

[3] Post Certificate Training and Education of Nurses. Report of the Standing Nursing Advisory Committee, Ministry of Health. May 1966.

SUGGESTION FOR FURTHER READING

"An Educated Heart," Kevin Mooney, M.P.S. *International Nursing Review,* Vol. 12, No. 5. September/October 1965.

SUGGESTIONS FOR FURTHER STUDY

1. *Middle Management*
With the help of a Principal Tutor, work out the essentials for a one week Refresher Course for Ward Sisters of over five years' experience.

2. *First Level Management*
Enumerate the "learning situations" which occur each day in the Ward, how can they be used to advantage?

CHAPTER 12

PROFESSIONAL RESPONSIBILITIES

WHAT IS A PROFESSION?

NURSES often talk glibly about "belonging to a profession", but on further questioning are sometimes unable to prove that they really understand what this means—or entails. Such words as "dedication" and "vocation" are used, but they do not in themselves indicate the difference between nursing and any other job. Dr. Marie Jahoda described this most ably when speaking at the International Council of Nurses in 1961, "A profession," she said, "implies that the quality of work done by its members, is of greater importance, and a source of greater satisfaction in their own eyes and the eyes of society, than the economic rewards they earn." This does not mean that the rewards should not reflect the quality of the work done, nor the responsibility which is undertaken; but it does mean that the nurse, in her service for others, recognises the value of every human being as an end in itself, and not as a means to an end.

A profession undertakes to maintain standards that will protect the good of the community, and it may introduce safeguards so that this may be achieved. It also undertakes to protect its members, to give security in situations when legal advice may be required, and to provide the opportunity to further professional knowledge. In nursing, this may be through a recognised organisation built up by the members themselves, such as the Royal College of Nursing.

Briefly, therefore, there are three aspects of professional life to be considered—the service to the community, standards to protect the public, and the protection of the member.

1. SERVICE TO THE COMMUNITY

The Nursing Profession enjoys a place of affection among the public, and is respected. This has been created through the years, by those who have worked in hospitals and in the community. It is a heritage handed on to the members to accept—or reject. If nurses wish to belong to this profession, therefore, there is an obligation to uphold the values and standards which have come to be part of its make-up. Nobody expects to join a society or club without accepting the rules; if nurses "adopt" their profession through qualification for entry, they also undertake the responsibilities which this entails.

What is it that the public respects in a nurse, which must be preserved? It can be summed up in the phrase "personal standards". This means how nurses present themselves, their self-respect, and self-control, and their awareness of the dignity of the individual. If people see this, they feel assured that these qualities will be extended to themselves in the form of discretion, courtesy, and human understanding. They will also feel confident in the knowledge that those who care for them have mastered technical skills and have acquired the necessary theoretical background. Much time is spent in considering the "image" of the profession, and it is no longer possible for nurses to escape publicity in the modern world of television and newspapers. Whether or not it is the right image is largely in their own hands. They need to inform the public of what they are doing and thinking, and to make the effort to put these thoughts on paper. Hitherto, there has been a certain lack of stimulus, and it has even sometimes been considered unethical. The important factor is the motive behind the publicity, and the integrity with which it is done.

Sometimes nurses have been unaware of how much damage can be caused to their reputation through their own internal conflicts. Writing in the *International Nursing Review*, Thelma Ingles, looking at nursing practice, says, "As the leaders in education and service begin to work together more harmoniously, they will be able, through their own behaviour, to encourage more effective relations between other members of the health team."[1] This is the "corporate responsibility" of which Florence Nightingale spoke, a unity of purpose which looks beyond individual preferences and prejudices, to the patient and the good of the organisation as a whole. This is the kind of unity which can give strength to the profession.

2. STANDARDS TO PROTECT THE PUBLIC

A good deal has already been said about personal standards and how these affect professional life. Of necessity, they also affect the people who are served. Nurses need to review continually their practice and that of those for whom they are responsible, to make sure that standards are maintained in every circumstance. It is not only important to protect the patient from physical harm, but the nurse is sometimes the only person who can protect him from emotional or psychological trauma. In an age which more and more disregards the privacy of the individual, and allows much of our personal lives to be broadcast or divulged through the press— even if with consent—it can be forgotten that personal feelings are easily hurt. In an anxiety to pursue research and the progress of medicine, the patient himself can be overlooked. Stanley Holder, in a recent paper given at the World Congress of Catholic Nurses, states, "The nurse must provide support when he (the patient) is

most dependent, encouragement when there is despair, and comfort when there is loneliness—all this in such a way that the
patient's rights as a person are safeguarded, and his human dignity
preserved."[2] In this technological age, it is so easy for the patient
to become obscured in a maze of well-meaning projects and ideas;
it is the duty of the nursing profession to have the courage to make
a stand wherever his feelings and needs as a person are endangered.

3. THE PROTECTION OF THE MEMBER

Since all who read this book will either be in positions of leadership or preparing to undertake them, they should be conversant
with the benefits to be obtained from membership of their professional organisation. No nurse can afford to be without the
security of legal indemnity in these days when litigation is not un-
common.[3]

Nurses are becoming more aware of the necessity to be conversant with the law as it affects their work but do not always realise
how, on occasions, they can quite innocently lay themselves open
to criticism. A recent article in the *American Journal Of Nursing*
shows how a nurse may undertake a procedure on being given the
assurance that another person (in this instance the doctor) will
take the responsibility, and find that, in fact, she cannot be
exonerated if there is a claim of negligence. "No one, no matter
how willing, or in what relationship he stands, can assume another's responsibility and thus free that other from liability for his
acts."[4] The moral behind this is surely to warn nurses not to take
unreasonable risks, and to be quite certain that they know which
procedures are beyond their province. The importance of the
Medico-Nursing Liaison Committee, which discusses duties which
can be termed "border-line", has already been mentioned, and a
similar link has been formed between the Royal College of Nursing
and the British Medical Association. However, organisations of this
nature are also necessary at local level.

Earlier in this chapter, reference was made to the importance of
financial reward reflecting the quality of the work done and the
responsibility it entails. Those who wish to study in detail the
procedure for negotiating salaries can refer to books on the subject,
but all nurses should know what is meant by Whitleyism, and how
the Whitley Council began. The Whitley Committee—named after
the Chairman the Right Hon. J. H. Whitley, M.P.—was inaugur-
ated in 1916 to investigate the system of collective bargaining then
in existence. As a result of these investigations, the Committee proposed "the establishment for each industry of an organisation,
representative of employers and workpeople to have as its object the
regular consideration of matters affecting the progress and well-

being of the industry from the point of view of all those engaged in it, so far as this is consistent with the general interest of the community."[5] As a result, Joint Industrial (Whitley) Councils were established in Industry, but it was not until the National Health Service was in operation that the Government, now being responsible for its employees in hospital and public health fields, set up the Whitley Councils for Nurses and Midwives, and for all other workers in the Service (1948).

The Nurses and Midwives Whitley Council consists of a Management and Staff side like all the other Councils, and the Staff side is represented by Professional Organisations and Trade Unions. It is important, therefore, that nurses, as members of a profession, realise that it is through the membership of their organisation that they have representation on the negotiating body which decides their salaries and conditions of service. All too often there is grumbling and grievance from the very people who do not bother to support those who are doing all the work.

This short description of the Whitley Council may have appeared to digress from the main theme of this chapter, but is in fact most relevant. Nurse leaders in the profession have a responsibility to see that nurses understand the machinery which exists for their financial welfare and conditions of service.

PROFESSIONAL OBLIGATIONS AND DAILY LIFE

Before leaving the subject, it may be helpful to consider what belonging to a profession means in terms of the daily routine and its demands. All qualified nurses should have considered this, and have reached conclusions which will stand the test when they meet the trials and difficulties which are part of everyday life. They must also be able to explain their thoughts to others.

1. *The Nurse-Patient Relationship.* Reference has already been made in the chapter on "Communications" to the nurse and her relationship with patients. The importance of what is said, how it is said, and the assurance which can come from personal contact have all been noted. Young nurses, however, often find it hard to know how far they can go, and before they know what is happening, they have become "involved" to an extent which makes it difficult for them. Perhaps they can best be helped by explaining that their skill and support needs to be shared by *all* their patients and that, if too much is given in one direction, there will be nothing left in another. It is the "helping all round" which keeps the balance. They must be encouraged to see this relationship as a temporary one, a professional relationship existing for a purpose. It is essential that this is the *right* purpose—that of assisting the

patient back to health. Patients rely on the nurse's consistency, and they quickly lose confidence if they see this failing.

Some people think that, in order to witness the suffering and sometimes tragic circumstances of some of their patients, nurses have to become hard. Nothing could be further from the truth, provided that the nurse has worked out a philosophy for life which recognises the part she is playing—to cure sometimes . . . to comfort always.

2. *Facing the Crisis.* When someone faces a crisis in their life, it puts to the test their ability to command the situation. This could be described as "emotional lifemanship". It is not only the degree of maturity which counts, but also the extent to which the individual has given thought to the deeper questions of life—and found some kind of answer. Why do people suffer? Should a patient know that he is going to die? Why do people die when they are still young? Nurses must contend with such problems in order that they can provide support and guidance in some form to those who may seek their help.

This philosophy can often be demonstrated best by the way the nurse herself handles a crisis when it comes along. She can show that understanding herself is one of the most helpful ways of understanding other people. There is a danger, however, that, in projecting her own reactions into the situation, she may find herself deciding how the other person should respond in his predicament. It is also important that false hopes are not offered in an effort to give support, and to release patients and relatives from some of their suffering.

In all these circumstances, the professional nurse must respect the religious beliefs of her patients. She becomes familiar with the hospital team which disregards creed when working at the bedside of a patient. There may be a Presbyterian Doctor, a Catholic Nurse, a Hindu and a Jew, but this does not make any difference to their performance as a living unit with one purpose. When she is nursing her patient, however, she cannot ignore this, for it may make a difference to the wishes of that person regarding his care and his future.

Advances in modern medicine have brought such matters as the treatment for Cardiac Arrest into the everyday lives of nurses. There has been much written on this subject, and nurses must have realised the ethical implications. It is when these questions arise that they find the need for an ethical code, which has its root in the professional thinking of every individual. The International Code of Nursing Ethics will be helpful, and should be familiar to all nurses; but unless there has been a *personal* acceptance of all that this means, nurses will be unable to interpret its contents as they meet the problems day by day.

In summing up a somewhat difficult subject, an attempt has been made to prove that professional needs are real, and that it is necessary to understand and accept them as a means of giving the highest standard of service. Nurses, through their own ability to face the problems and catastrophies caused by illness and suffering, can enable others to face them too. It is a question of keeping the water out of the ship in order that others may be steered to the land. Every navigator, however, needs a chart to guide him.

REFERENCES

[1] "A concept of Nursing Practice." *International Nursing Review*, April 1966, Vol. 13, No. 2.

[2] "The Nurse and her Contribution to World Unity," S. Holder. *Nursing Times*, 22.7.66, p. 968.

[3] *For Your Protection*, Royal College of Nursing and National Council of Nurses of the United Kingdom.

[4] "The Law and The Nurse," N. Hershey. *American Journal of Nursing*, May 1966, Vol. 66, No. 5, p. 1053.

[5] *The Nurses and Midwives Whitley Council*, Royal College of Nursing, Public Health Section.

SUGGESTIONS FOR FURTHER READING

"The Professional Ethic," Norah Mackenzie, M.A. *International Nursing Review*, August 1966, Vol. 13, No. 4.

"Code of Ethics as applied to Nursing." *International Nursing Review*, Nov./Dec. 1965, Vol. 12, No. 6, p. 38.

Decisions about Life and Death. A Problem in Modern Medicine. Published by Church Information Office for the Church Assembly Board for Social Responsibility, 1965.

"Care of the Dying," Dr. Cicely Saunders. *Nursing Times*. Reprint. Published by Macmillan & Co. Ltd., London.

CHAPTER 13

THE PATTERN OF THE FUTURE

AMIDST the pressures of everyday life, it is easy to become pre-occupied with the present, and to leave the future to take care of itself. On the other hand, future policy emerges through the efforts of those prepared to re-examine themselves, their attitudes and their practices in the light of everyday events. This takes courage, since new avenues have to be explored, often in the face of opposition. It also requires wisdom to decide which factors are impeding progress and must therefore be set aside, and which are to be safeguarded and preserved.

This "critical thinking" must begin within the Schools of Nursing: "If nursing students are to be fully prepared to face a future of change, a problem-solving approach should be adopted from the beginning of their education. Students taught in this way will be challenged to think; they will learn to seek answers for themselves, rather than to rely on someone else's experience, or on the memorisation of facts; they will be able to continue their inquiring attitude as they graduate and enter employment."[1] Only in this way can the nursing profession be sure that it will have lively and confident members coming forward to make their contribution.

The pattern of the future can only be a shadowy outline, but nurses can be certain that their responsibilities will take them beyond the confines of the hospital, as the concept of "nursing" widens to include not only patient care, but the total health needs of the community.

These changes are taking place at a time when the advances of medical science are challenging the skill of the nurse and facing her with problems hitherto unknown. "A phenomenon that nurses must look upon with great apprehension, is the lack of balance between, on the one hand, the medical and technical advances as regards diagnosis and therapy, and on the other, the development of basic nursing care, which is traditionally their main function."[2] In reconsidering her role, the nurse must be sure that she continues to provide what the patient really requires. The booklet *Basic Principles of Nursing Care*[3] reminds the profession that nursing has its roots in *fundamental* human needs.

All these factors have an impact on the practice of nursing and will also affect its teaching. The management of hospitals and nurse training schools must therefore be such that nurses can be ready to meet the demands which will be made upon them. This is the "enabling" process which is the foundation of all successful administration. It means that, although the scientific tools of management must be employed and understood, they cannot suffice by themselves. This can only come if leaders in the profession at all levels, have a deep understanding of human needs, and the will to meet them; and this must be combined with personal and intellectual integrity. The latter has been described as the quality on which all other qualities of leadership are based—"the thing that makes people trust you".[4]

REFERENCES

[1] W.H.O. Expert Committee On Nursing 5th Report. W.H.O. Technical Report Series, No. 347, Geneva, 1966.

[2] "The Nurse's Role Tomorrow," Brita Asplund. *International Nursing Review*, Vol. 13, No. 6, December 1966.

[3] *Basic Principles of Nursing Care*, Virginia Henderson. International Council of Nurses.

[4] Field-Marshal Sir William Slim, "Leadership," an address given in 1953 later published by the Sydney Division, Australian Institute of Management.

APPENDIX A

SELECTION OF PERSONNEL

A. *Physical* B. *Psychological*

Individual
$\begin{cases} \text{1. Fitness} \\ \text{2. Talents} \\ \text{3. Attainments} \\ \text{4. Interests} \end{cases}$ $\begin{cases} \text{General} \\ \text{Special} \end{cases}$
$\begin{cases} \text{1. Fitness} \\ \text{2. Temperament} \\ \text{3. Attitudes} \\ \text{4. Disposition} \end{cases}$

C. *Circumstances*

FIRST CONSIDER THE JOB, AND THE QUALIFICATIONS REQUIRED

A. *Physical*
1. *Fitness*
   (a) Is she physically suited to the job?
   (b) Appearance—manner—first impressions.

2. *Talents*
   (a) Has she the ability to undertake the work and make it a success?
   (b) Has she had the right preparation for the job?
   (c) General intelligence?
   (d) Mental and manual dexterity?

3. *Attainments*
   Degrees, qualifications, and certificates.
   Past experience (are there any unexplained gaps in the dates?).

4. *Interests*
   (a) Is she interested in people?
   (b) Other interests and hobbies.

B. *Psychological*
1. *Fitness*
   (a) Is there a vocational approach to the job?
   (b) Is there a general interest and desire to take part?

2. *Temperament*
>   Does this appear to be equable—has she shown stability so far?

3. *Attitudes*
>   (a) Has she a broad-minded approach to people and problems?
>   (b) Is there a willingness to accept responsibility?
>   (c) Is she a good mixer?

4. *Disposition*
>   (a) Will this person fit into the situation and be acceptable?
>   (b) Has she ability to influence others—has she shown qualities of leadership?

C. *Circumstances*
>   (a) Geographical—is the place of work congenial, and convenient?
>   (b) Family situation—are there particular problems and responsibilities?
>   (c) Has there been parental approval? (for persons under age).

AVOID

Personal prejudices.

Enable the candidate to talk—don't talk too much yourself.

Avoid asking questions which can be answered with a "yes" or "no".

REMEMBER

To tell the candidate the conditions and terms of the job, and make sure they are understood.

Let her know when to expect to hear the result of the interview.

If previously employed, find out how much notice has to be given, and whether annual leave is up to date.

Make sure the candidate has an opportunity to ask questions, visit the department or hospital, meet people, and see the residential accommodation if necessary.

APPENDIX B

REPORT WRITING

Three rules for writing a report for a Committee:

1. Preparation must be done first—make sure it is quite clear what is required and why.
2. Be clear, concise and convincing.
3. State facts in a logical sequence and support them with evidence and statistics as necessary.

EXAMPLE

An addition to the Nursing Establishment is required in order to provide nursing services for an Intensive Care Unit in a 600 bedded hospital.

Preparation

1. Ascertain the number of patients who are likely to be nursed in the Unit at any one time.

2. Work out, in consultation with the Sister who is to be in charge, the number and grades of nursing staff required to provide a 24 hour nursing service. Points to remember:

   (a) Define the duties and responsibilities of each grade.
   (b) A shift system of duty will be required.
   (c) The Unit will need to be self-sufficient for holiday and sick-ness relief, night duty, etc., because of the specialised nature of the work.

3. Consult with the medical officer in charge to find out if there are any special requirements for this particular Unit over and above the normal which will necessitate additional staff.

4. Consider the number and grades of supporting staff.

5. Take into account any external problems which may in-fluence the number of staff needed, e.g.: geographical location of the Unit, quality of supporting services, etc.

6. Evaluate any staff economies which can be made.

Framework of the Report

Every attempt to convince a Committee in writing should follow a pattern which will enable members to read the material easily, and grasp the main points. State clearly at the beginning the main substance of the Report:

Introduction

An Intensive Care Unit of 6 beds is to be opened on 20th June this year. The Sister-in-Charge has already been appointed (see last month's report), but additional members of staff will be required necessitating a revision of the nursing establishment.

A. *Advantages of having an Intensive Care Unit*

1. Acutely ill patients requiring specialised nursing care can be grouped together enabling a better service to be given in ideal surroundings.

2. The hospital is shortly to become an Accident Centre and there will be an increasing number of patients requiring this special care.

3. Some economies may be made in the numbers of staff required, if the very ill patients are not scattered throughout the hospital.

B. *Effect of the Opening of this Unit on Nursing Service Needs*

1. Whilst it will be possible to provide better facilities for the patients, the use of complicated machinery will increase the need for highly trained nurses with special technical skills.

2. Because of the specialised nature of the work, the establishment will need to include provision for night duty, and nurses for "relief".

C. *Steps taken to meet these demands*

1. Appointment of Sister-in-Charge with previous experience of a Ward of this nature.

2. Secondment of a Ward Sister to an established Unit for two months' concentrated training.

3. A plan of In-service training has been drawn up with the help of the Tutors and Clinical Instructor.

4. Supporting staff are being recruited, including a Ward Clerk.

D. *Estimated Number of Additional Nursing Staff Required*

It is expected that a saving of 2 Full-time Staff Nurses will be made by grouping the patients.

Total Staff Establishment for Intensive Care Unit:	Sister-in-Charge
	Ward Sister
	x Staff Nurses
	x Enrolled Nurses
Therefore Additional Staff Required:	x Nursing Auxiliaries
	x Staff Nurses
	x Enrolled Nurses
	x Nursing Auxiliaries

Total Cost £............

(Present Whitley Council Scales)

Would the Committee please agree to this increase so that vacancies may be advertised within the hospital and in the Nursing Press.

Signed ....

Date ....

NOTES

A certain amount of detail is required since it is possible that a lay committee may not know the function of an Intensive Care Unit. Be prepared to elaborate and answer questions. Have details of present nursing establishment available.

APPENDIX C

GUIDANCE NOTES FOR NURSING AUXILIARIES

In welcoming you to this hospital, it may be useful to have these notes to help you to understand the part you will play in the nursing team.

Your duties will bring you into close contact with the patients. You will be shown how to observe them as you attend to their needs, and it will be a great help to the nursing and medical staff if you let them know of any change in the patient's behaviour or general appearance that you may notice. For example, such things as loss of appetite in a patient who normally eats well, complaints of pain, or when a patient who is usually cheerful seems "out of sorts".

Working under supervision as part of the ward team, you will be able to help the nursing staff with the following duties:

Patients in Bed
    (a) Care of pressure areas, and moving patients in bed.
    (b) Changing of linen and bed-making.
    (c) Helping with general toilet.
    (d) Helping with meals, preparing trays, and feeding patients.

Patients who are out of Bed
    (a) Assisting patients to the toilet.
    (b) Helping them to walk or perform simple exercises.
    (c) Accompanying patients to other departments.
    (d) Helping with meals, and giving assistance and encouragement with diversional therapy.

THINGS TO REMEMBER

Information about Patients. This is always kept in strict confidence. Those who care for patients must see that nothing that is learnt about them, or their illness, is discussed outside the Ward or Department.

Accidents. It is also important to see that patients come to no harm. If an accident does occur to a patient, or to a member of the staff, this must be reported *immediately* to the Sister or Nurse-in-Charge at that time.

Patient's Property. Whilst the Hospital Authorities do not accept responsibility for patient's property, unless it is handed over and a receipt obtained, care must be taken to see that belongings do not go astray.

If you are in doubt at any time, do not be afraid to ask for help. We hope you will be very happy, and find satisfaction in the contribution you will give.

INDEX

111